Mahmoud Darwish

Why Did You
Leave the Horse Alone?

Translated from the Arabic by Jeffrey Sacks

archipelago books

Limadha tarakta al-hisan wahidan first published by Riad al-Rayyes, Ltd.
© Mahmoud Darwish, 1995

First Archipelago Books edition, 2006
Fourth Printing

Archipelago Books
232 Third Street, #A111
Brooklyn, NY 11215
www.archipelagobooks.org

Library of Congress Cataloging-in-Publication Data
Darwish, Mahmud.
[Li-madha tarakta al-hisan wahidan. English]
Why did you leave the horse alone? / by Mahmoud Darwish ;
translated from Arabic by Jeffrey Sacks.—1st ed.
p. cm.
isbn 0-9763950-1-0 (alk. paper)
I. Sacks, Jeffrey. II. Title.
pj7820.a7l513 2006
892.7'16—dc22   2005035484

Distributed to the trade by Penguin Random House
www.penguinrandomhouse.com

The edition of the Koran quoted in this volume is *The Koran Interpreted*,
translated by Arthur J. Arberry, Oxford World Classics, Oxford
University Press, 1998.

Cover art: *Don't Forsake the Steed*, Tamam Al Akhal

This publication was made possible with the support of Lannan Foundation
and the New York State Council on the Arts, a state agency.

PRINTED IN THE UNITED STATES OF AMERICA

Translator's Acknowledgments

If the translation of poetry may seem to be an act carried out by a solitary individual, this is so only insofar as one will never have lingered with a poem alone. I wish to thank Leila Zacharia for listening to early drafts of some of the translations in this volume. I wish to thank Suhail Shadoud, Maged Zaher, and Sinan Antoon for taking the time to read and comment on the manuscript, and for helping to untie knots. I wish to thank Ammiel Alcalay for reading the manuscript and for offering suggestions. I wish to thank Elias Khoury for generously taking the time to offer guidance and answer questions. I wish to thank Avital Ronell for her support and generosity. I wish to thank Jill Schoolman for her integrity, kindness, and keen editorial eyes and ears. I wish to thank my wife, Leah, for her support, encouragement, and friendship, and my daughter, Leila, for her kisses. Finally, I wish to thank Mahmoud Darwish, for his generosity, and for the poetic word that he has offered in this text and elsewhere.

In memory of those who are absent:

My grandfather, Husayn

My grandmother, Amina

My father, Salim

And for the one who is present:

Huriyya, my mother

Poems

Why Did You
Leave the Horse Alone?

I See my Ghost
Coming from a Distance

I look out like a balcony on what I want
I look out on my friends carrying the evening mail
wine and bread
novels and records . . .

I look out on a sea gull and on the trucks of soldiers
changing the trees of this place.

I look out on the dog of my neighbor who emigrated
from Canada a year and a half ago . . .

I look out on the name Abu al-Tayyib al-Mutanabbi
who traveled from Tiberius to Egypt
on the horse of song

I look out on the Persian rose that rises up
over the iron fence

I look out like a balcony on what I want

I look out on trees that guard the night from itself
and guard the sleep of those who want me dead . . .

أَرَى شَبَحي
قادِمًا من بعيد . . .

أُطِلُّ ، كَشُرْفَةِ بَيْتٍ ، على ما أُريدْ
أُطِلُّ عَلى أَصدقائي ، وهم يحملُون بريدَ
المساء : نبيذًا وخُبزًا ،
وبعضَ الروايات والأُسطوانات . . .

أُطِلُّ على نَوْرَس ، وعلى شاحناتِ جُنُودْ
تُغَيِّرُ أشجارَ هذا المكانْ .

أُطِلُّ على كَلْبِ جاري المُهاجِر
مِنْ كَنَدا ، منذ عامٍ ونصف . . .

أُطِلُّ على اسم «أَبي الطَّيِّب المُتَنَبِّي» ،
المُسافِر من طبريًا إلى مصر
فوق حصانِ النشيدْ

أُطِلُّ على الوَرْدَة الفارسيَّة تصعُدُ
فوقَ سياجِ الحديدْ

أُطِلُّ ، كشُرْفَةِ بَيْتٍ ، على ما أُريدْ

أُطِلُّ على شَجَرٍ يحرُسُ اللَّيلَ من نَفْسِه
ويحرس نَوْمَ الذين يُحبُّونني مَيِّتًا . . .

I look out on the wind searching for its homeland
in itself . . .

I look out on a woman sunbathing within herself . . .

I look out over the procession of ancient prophets
climbing barefoot to Jerusalem
I ask: Is there a new prophet
for this new time?

I look out like a balcony on what I want

I look out on my image fleeing from itself
to the stone staircase, carrying my mother's scarf
trembling in the wind: What would happen, were I to return
to childhood? And I to you . . . and you to me

I look out on the trunk of an olive tree that hid Zakariyya
I look out on words that have died out in *Lisan al-Arab*

I look out on the Persians, the Byzantines, the Sumerians
and the new refugees . . .

I look out on the necklace of one of the poor women of Tagore
ground beneath the carriage of the handsome prince . . .

I look out on a hoopoe sapped from the king's reprimand

I look out on a hoopoe sapped from the king's reprimand

أُطِلُّ على الرّيحِ تبحثُ عن وَطنٍ الريحِ
في نفسِها . . .

أُطِلُّ على امرأةٍ تَتَشَمَّسُ في نفسِها . . .

أُطِلُّ على موكبِ الأنبياء القُدامى
وهم يَصعَدُون حُفاةً إلى أُورشليم
وأسألُ : هَل من نَبيٍّ جَديدٍ
لهذا الزمان الجَديدِ؟

أُطِلُّ ، كشُرفةِ بيْتٍ ، على ما أُريدْ
أُطِلُّ على صورَتي وهْيَ تهرب من نفسِها
إلى السُّلَّمِ الحجريِّ ، وتحمل منديل أُمّي
وتخفق في الريح : ماذا سيحدث لو عُدْتُ
طفلاً؟ وعدتُ إليكِ . . . وعدتِ إليَّ

أُطِلُّ على جذعِ زيتونةٍ خبَّأتْ زكريّا
أُطِلُّ على المُفرداتِ الّتي انقَرَضَتْ في «لسان العَرَبْ»

أُطِلُّ على الفُرْس ، والروم ، والسومريَّين ،
واللاجئينَ الجُدُدْ . . .

أُطِلُّ على عِقْدِ إحدَى فقيراتِ طاغورَ
تطحنُهُ عَرَبَاتُ الأمير الوسيمْ . . .

أُطِلُّ على هُدْهُدٍ مُجهَدٍ من عتابِ الملك

I look out on metaphysics:

What will happen . . . What will happen after the ashes?

I look out on my body, afraid, from a distance . . .

I look out like a balcony on what I want

I look out on my language, two days later
A short absence is enough
for Aeschylus to open the door to peace
A short speech is enough
for Antonio to incite war
A hand of a woman in my hand
is enough
to embrace my freedom
and for the ebb and flow to begin anew in my body

I look out like a balcony on what I want

I look out on my ghost
coming
from
a distance . . .

أُطِلُّ على ما وراء الطبيعة :

ماذا سيحدث . . . ماذا سيحدث بعد الرماد؟

أُطِلُّ على جَسَدي خائفًا من بعيدْ . . .

أُطِلُّ ، كَشُرْفَةِ بَيْتٍ ، على ما أُريدْ

أُطِلُّ على لُغَتي بَعْدَ يَوْمَيْن . يكفي غِيابٌ
قليلٌ ليفتَحَ أَسْخيليْوُسُ البابَ للسِّلْم ،
يكفي
خِطابٌ قصير لِيُشعل أنطونيو الحربَ ،
تكفي
يَدُ امرأةٍ في يَدي
كي أُعانق حُرِّيَتي
وأن يبدأ المَدُّ والجَزْرُ في جَسَدي من جديدْ

أُطِلُّ ، كشُرفةِ بَيْتٍ ، على ما أُريدْ

أُطِلُّ على شَبَحي
قادمًا
من
بَعيدْ . . .

I.

Icons of the Place's Crystal

أَيقونات من بلَّوْرِ المكان

A Cloud in my Hand

They saddled the horses
They didn't know why
But they saddled the horses on the plain

The place was ready for his birth. A hill
of his ancestors' basil that looks east and west. An olive tree
near another in the holy books lifts the surfaces of language . . .
Azure smoke prepares the day for an affair
that concerns only God. March is
the pampered child of months. It combs cotton from the almond
tree. It gives a banquet of mallow to the church courtyard
March is a land for the swallow's night, and for a woman
preparing for her scream in the wilderness . . . stretching
across the oak trees

A child is born
His scream
in the cracks of the place

We parted at the steps of the house. They said:
In my scream there's a caution that doesn't suit the abandon of the plants

أَسْرَجُوا الخَيْلَ ،
لا يَعرفونَ لماذا ،
ولكنَّهُمْ أَسْرَجُوا الخيلَ في السهل

. . . كانَ المكانُ مُعَدًّا لِمَوْلِده : تلَّةً
من رياحين أجداده تَتَلَفَّتُ شَرْقًا وغَرْبًا . وزيتونةً
قُرْبَ زيتونَة في المَصَاحف تُعْلي سُطُوحَ اللُغَةْ . . .
ودُخَانًا من اللازَوَرْد يُؤَثِّثُ هذا النهارَ لمسْألَةٍ
لا تَخُصُّ سوى الله . آذارُ طفلُ
الشُّهور المُدَلَّلُ . آذارُ ينددُف قطنًا على شَجَر
اللَوْز . آذارُ يُولِمُ خُبَيزةً لفناء الكنيسة .
آذارُ أرضٌ لِلَيْلِ السُنُونو ، ولامرأة
تَسْتَعِدُّ لِصرخَتِها في البَراري . . . وتَمتدُّ في
شَجَر السَّنديانْ .

يُولَدُ الآنَ طفلٌ ،
وصرخَتُهُ ،
في شقوق المكانْ

إفترَقْنا على دَرَج البيت . كانوا يقولونَ :
في صَرخَتي حَذَرٌ لا يُلائمُ طَيْشَ النباتات ،

In my scream there's rain; did I wrong my brothers
when I said I saw angels playing with the wolf
in the courtyard? I don't remember
their names. And I don't remember the way they
spoke . . . or the way they lightly flew

My friends shimmer like the night without leaving
a trace behind them. Should I tell my mother the truth?
I have other brothers
Brothers who put a moon on my balcony
Brothers who weave, with their needles, a coat of daisies

They saddled the horses
They didn't know why
But they saddled the horses at the end of the night

. . . Seven sheaths of grain are enough for the summer table
Seven sheaths of grain in my hands. And in each grain
a wheat field makes another grow. My father
drew water from his well. Don't dry up, he
told it. He took me by the hand
to see how I'd grow like rose moss . . .
I walk at the edge of the well: I have two moons
one above

في صَرختي مَطَرٌ ؛ هَل أَسأتُ إلى إخوَتي
عندما قلتُ إنّي رأيتُ ملائكةً يَلعبونَ مع الذئب
في باحة الدَار؟ لا أتذكرُ
أسماءهُمْ . ولا أتذكّرُ أيضًا طريقتَهُمْ في
الكَلام . . . وفي خفّة الطيرانْ

أصدقائي يرفّون ليلاً ، ولا يتركونْ
خَلفَهُمْ أثرًا . هَل أقول لأمّي الحقيقةَ :
لِيْ إخوةٌ آخرونْ
إخوةٌ ينسجون بإبرتهم معطفَ الأُقحُوانْ

أسرَجوا الخَيلَ ،
لا يَعرفونَ لماذا ،
ولكنّهم أسرَجوا الخَيلَ في آخر اللّيل

. . .سَبعُ سَنابلَ تَكفي لمائدَة الصّيف .
سَبعُ سَنابلَ بَين يديَّ . وفي كُلّ سُنبُلَة
يُنبتُ الحقلُ حقلاً من القمح . كان
أبي يَسحبُ الماءَ من بئره ويقولُ
لَهُ : لا تَجفَّ . ويأخذني من يَديْ
لأرَى كيف أكبُرُ كالفَرْفحينة . . .
أمشي على حافّة البئر : لِيْ قَمران
واحدٌ في الأعالي

and another in the water, swimming . . . I have two moons
each certain, like their forefathers, of what is true

Of the sacred laws . . . they melted the swords' iron
into plows. The sword won't repair what
the summer spoils – they said. They prayed
for a long time. They sang their praises to nature . . .
But they saddled the horses
to dance their dance
on the night's silver . . .

A cloud in my hand wounds me. I don't
want from the earth more than
this earth: the scent of cardamom and hay
between my father and the horse
In my hand is a cloud that wounded me. But I
don't want from the sun more
than an orange seed and more than
the gold that flowed from the call to prayer

They saddled the horses
The didn't know why
But they saddled the horses
at the end of the night, and waited
for a ghost rising from the cracks of the place . . .

وآخرُ في الماء يسبَحْ . . . لِيْ قَمران ْ
واثقَين ، كأسلافهمْ ، من صَواب

الشرائع . . سَكُّوا حديدَ السُّيوف
محاريثَ . لن يُصلحَ السَّيفُ ما
أَفْسَدَ الصَّيْفُ – قالُوا . وصَلُّوا
طويلاً . وغَنُّوا مَدائحهمْ للطَّبيعَة . . .
لكنَّهُم أسْرَجوا الخَيلَ ،
كَي يَرْقُصُوا رَقْصَةَ الخَيْلِ ،
في فضَّة اللَّيلِ . . .

تُجَرّحُني غَيمةٌ في يدي : لا
أُريدُ منَ الأرض أكثَرَ منْ
هذه الأرض : رائَحة الهال والقَشِّ
بينَ أبي والحصانْ .
في يَدي غَيْمَةٌ جَرَحَتْني . ولكنَّني
لا أُريدُ من الشَّمس أكثَرَ
من حَبَّة البُرتقال وأكثرَ منْ
ذَهبٍ سالَ من كلمات الأذانْ

أَسْرَجوا الخَيْلَ ،
لا يَعرفونَ لماذا ،
ولكنَّهُمْ أَسرَجوا الخَيلَ
في آخر اللَّيل ، وانتظروا
شَبَحًا طالعًا من شُقوق المكانْ . . .

Innocent Villagers

I still didn't know my mother's customs or those of her family
when the trucks came from the sea. But I
knew the scent of tobacco on my grandfather's cloak
and the eternal scent of coffee, since I was born
as domesticated animals here are born –
with one push!

We, too, cry falling to the edge of
the earth. But we don't store our voices
in old jars. Nor hang mountain goats
on the wall. Nor claim the kingdom of dust
Nor do our dreams look out over the grapes of others
Nor do they break the rule!

My name didn't yet have its feathers, so I jumped, farther
in the afternoon. The heat of April was like
the fiddles of our passing visitors, making us fly like doves
My first warning bell: the attraction of a woman who seduces me
to smell the milk on her knees. So I run
from the banquet's sting!

قُرويُّونَ ، مِنْ غَيْر سُوء . .

لم أكُنْ بَعْدُ أعرفُ عادات أُمِّي ، ولا أهلَها
عندَما جاءَت الشّاحناتُ منَ البحر . لكنّني
كُنتُ أعرفُ رائحةَ التَّبغ حول عباءَة جدّي
ورائحةَ القهوَة الأبدِيَّة ، منذ وُلدتُ
كما يُولَدُ الحَيَوانُ الأليفُ هُنا
دفعةً واحدةً!

نَحنُ أيضًا لنا صَرْخَةٌ في الهُبوط إلى حافَّةِ
الأرض . لكنّنا لا نُخَزّنُ أصواتَنا
في الجرار العَتيقة . لا نشنق الوَعْلَ
فوق الجدار ، ولا نَدّعي مَلَكُوت الغبار ،
وأحْلامُنا لا تُطِلُّ عَلى عنَب الآخرين ،
ولا تَكْسِرُ القاعِدَةْ!

لَم يكُن بعدُ لاسميَ ريشٌ فأقفز أبعَد
بعدَ الظهيرَة . كانت حرارَةُ إبريلَ مثل
رباباتٍ زُوّارنا العابرينَ تطيِّرُنا كالحمامات .
لي جَرَسٌ أوَّلُ : جاذبيَّةُ أُنثى تُراوغُني
لأشمَّ الحليبَ عَلى ركبتيها ، فأهرب
مِن لَسعة المائدةْ!

We also have our secret when the sun falls
across the white poplar trees: a desire to cry over someone
who died, who died for nothing, grips us
A passion to visit Babylon, or a mosque in Damascus,
seizes us. A tear of the pigeons' coo in the
tale of eternal pain sheds us!

Innocent villagers who don't regret
their words. Our names, like our days, are alike
Our names don't identify us entirely. We slip
between the words of guests. We have much to tell about
the land to the stranger as she sews her scarf feather by
feather from the space of our returning birds!

The place didn't have nails stronger than the chinaberry
when the trucks came from the sea. We were
preparing our cattle's feed in their stalls, ordering
our days in cupboards made by our hands,
searching for the horse's affection, gesturing towards
the fugitive star.

We also got on the trucks. The glow of emeralds
spoke to us through the night of our olive tree. The barking of

نحن أيضًا لنا سرُّنا عندما تقعُ الشَّمسُ
عن شجَرِ الحَوْر : تخطفُنا رغبةً في البكاء
على أحدٍ ماتَ من أجلِ شيءٍ لا شيءَ ماتَ ،
وتجرفُنا صَبْوَةٌ لزيارة بابلَ أو جامع
في دمشقَ ، وتذرفُنا دمعةً من هَدِيل
اليمامات في سيرة الوجع الخالدةْ!

قرويُّونَ ، مِن غيرِ سوءٍ ، ولا نَدَم
في الكلامِ . وأسماؤُنا مثلُ أيَّامنا تتشابهُ ،
أسماؤُنا لا تَدُلُّ عَلينا تمامًا . ونَنْدَسُ
بينَ حديثِ الضّيوفِ . لَنَا ما نَقولُ عَن
الأرضِ للأجنبيّة حينَ تُطرِّزُ منديلَها ريشةً
ريشةً من فضاء عصافيرنا العائدةْ!

لَم تكن للمكانِ مساميرُ أقوى من الزنزلَخْتِ
عندما جاءَتِ الشّاحناتُ من البَحرِ . كنّا
نهيِّئُ وجبةَ أبقارِنا في حظائرِها ، ونرتِّبُ
أيَّامَنا في خزائنَ من شُغْلِنا اليدويِّ
ونخطبُ وُدَّ الحصانِ ، ونُومئُ
للنّجمةِ الشاردةْ .

نحنُ أيضًا صعدنا إلى الشّاحنات . يُسامِرُنا
لَمعانُ الزُّمُرُّد في لَيْلِ زَيْتونِنا ، ونُباحُ

dogs at a fleeting moon over the church tower
But we weren't afraid. Because our childhood didn't
come with us. A song was enough for us: We'll return
in a little while, to our house . . . when the trucks empty
their extra load!

كلاب على قَمَر عابر فوقَ بُرْج الكنيسة ،
لكنَّنا لم نكن خائفينَ . لأنَّ طفولتنا لم
تجِئْ معنا . واكتفينا بأغنيَّة : سوفَ نرجعُ
عمَّا قليل إلى بيتنا . . . عندما تُفْرِغُ الشَّاحناتُ
حُمُولَتَها الزائدَةُ!

The Owl's Night

Here is a present that yesterday doesn't touch . . .
When we reached
the last of the trees we noticed that we
were no longer able to notice. When
we looked at the trucks. We saw absence
heaping up its selected things and pitching
its eternal tent around us . . .

Here is a present
that yesterday doesn't touch
Silk thread slips between the mulberry trees
letters on the night's notebook. Only
butterflies light our boldness
descending to the hollow of strange words:
Was this difficult man my father?
Perhaps I'll look after myself here. Perhaps
I'll give birth, now, to myself, with myself
and choose for my name vertical letters . . .

Here is a present
sitting in time's emptiness, staring
at the trace of those who pass on the river's reeds

لَيْلَة البُوم

ههُنا حاضرٌ لا يُلامسُهُ الأمسُ . . .
حين وَصَلْنا
إلى آخر الشَّجَرات انتبهنا إلى أَنَّنا
لم نَعُدْ قادرينَ على الانتباه . وحين
التفتْنَا إلى الشّاحنات رأينا الغيابَ
يُكَدِّسُ أشياءَه المُنْتَقَاةَ ، وينصبُ
خيمَتَهُ الأبديَّةَ من حولنا . . .

ههُنا حاضرٌ
لا يُلامسة الأمسُ ،
ينسَلُّ من شَجَر التُّوت خيطُ الحرير
حروفًا على دفتَر اللَّيل . لا شيءَ
غيرَ الفَراش يُضيءُ جَسارتَنا في
النُزول إلى حُفرَة الكلمات الغريبةِ :
هَل كان هذا الشقيُّ أبي؟
ربّما أتدبَّرُ أَمْري هُنا . ربّما
أَلدُّ الآن نَفسي بنَفسي ،
وأَختارُ لاسمي حروفًا عموديَّةً . . .

ههُنا حاضرٌ
جالسٌ في خلاء الأَواني يُحَدِّقُ
في أَثَر العابرين على قَصَب النَّهر ،

polishing their flutes with wind . . . Perhaps speech
will become transparent, so we'll see windows in it, open
Perhaps time will hurry, with us
carrying our tomorrow in its luggage . . .

Here is a present
without time
No one here found anyone who remembered
how we left the door, a gust of wind. Or anyone who remembered
when we fell off yesterday. Yesterday
shattered over the floor, shrapnel gathered together
by others, like mirrors for their image, after us . . .

Here is a present
without place
Perhaps I'll look after myself and scream at
the owl's night: Was that difficult man
my father, who would have me carry the burden of his history?
Perhaps I'll transform within my name and choose
my mother's words and habits as it should
be: She'll be able to joke with me
whenever salt touches my blood. She'll be able
to comfort me whenever a nightingale bites my mouth!

يصقُلُ ناياتِهم بالهواءِ . . لعلَّ الكلامَ
يشفُّ فنبصِر فيه النوافذَ مفتوحةً ،
ولعلَّ الزمان يحثُّ الخُطى معنا
حاملاً غَدَنا في حقائبه . . .

ههُنا حاضرٌ
لا زمانَ لَهُ ،
لم يَجِدْ أحَدٌ ، ههُنا ، أحَدًا يتذكَّرُ
كيف خرجنا من البابِ ، ريحًا ، وفي
أيِّ وقتٍ وَقَعْنا عن الأمس فانكسَرَ
الأمسُ فوق البلاط شظايا يُرَكِّبها
الآخرون مرايا لِصُوَرتِهِمْ بعدنا . . .

ههُنا حاضرٌ
لا مكانَ لهُ ،
رُبَّما أتدبَّرُ أمري ، وأصرخ في
ليلة البُوم : هَلْ كان ذاك الشقيُّ
أبي ، كي يُحَمِّلَني عبءَ تاريخِه؟
رُبَّما أتغيَّرُ في اسمي ، وأختارُ
ألفاظَ أُمِّي وعاداتِها مثلما ينبغي
أن تكون : كأنْ تستطيع مُداعَبَتي
كُلَّما مسَّ ملحٌ دمي ، وكأنْ تستطيع
مُعالَجتي كلَّما عَضَّني بلبلٌ في فمي!

Here is a present
fleeting
Here strangers hung their guns on
the branches of an olive tree, prepared dinner
quickly from tin cans, and left
quickly for their trucks . . .

ههُنا حاضرٌ

عابِرٌ ،

ههُنا علَّقَ الغُرَباءُ بنادقَهُمْ فَوْقَ

أغصان زَيْتُونَة ، وأَعدُّوا عشاءً

سريعًا من العلَبِ المعدنيَّة ، وانطلقوا

مسرعين إلى الشَّاحنات . . .

The Eternity of Cactus

– Where are you taking me, father?
– Where the wind takes us, my son . . .

. . . As the two were leaving the plain where
Bonaparte's soldiers surveyed
the shadows on the old wall of Acre –
a father said to his son: Don't be afraid. Don't
be afraid of the drone of bullets! Stay close
to the ground so you'll survive! We'll survive and climb
a mountain in the north and return when
the soldiers return to their distant families

– Who will live in the house after us,
father?
– It will remain as it is, as it has always been,
my son!

He felt for his key the way he would feel for
his limbs and was reassured. He said
as they climbed through a fence of thorns:
Remember, my son, here the British crucified
your father on the thorns of a cactus for two nights
and he didn't confess. You will grow up,
my son, and tell those who inherit their guns
the story of the blood upon the iron . . .

بَدُ الصُّبَّار

إلى أَينَ تَأْخُذُني يا أَبي؟
إلى جِهَةِ الرَّيحِ يا وَلَدي . . .

. . . وَهُما يَخْرُجانِ مِنَ السَهْلِ ، حَيْثُ
أَقام جنودُ بونابرتَ تَلاًّ لِرَصْدِ
الظلالِ على سورِ عَكَّا القَديمْ-
يقولُ أَبٌ لابنهِ : لا تَخَفْ . لا
تَخَفْ من أَزيزِ الرَّصاصِ! إلتصِقْ
بالتُرابِ لتنجو! سننجُو ونعلو على
جَبَلٍ في الشَّمالِ ، ونرجعُ حينَ
يعودُ الجنودُ إلى أَهلهم في البعيدْ

- ومَن يسكُنُ البَيْتَ من بَعدِنا
يا أَبي؟
- سيبقَى على حالِهِ مثلما كان
يا وَلَدي!

تَحَسَّسَ مفتاحَهُ مثلما يتحسَّسُ
أَعضاءَهُ ، واطمأَنَّ . وقال لَهُ
وهما يعبُرانِ سياجًا من الشوكِ :
يا ابني تذكَّرْ! هُنا صَلَبَ الإنجليزُ
أَباكَ عَلى شَوْكِ صُبّارةٍ ليلتينِ ،
ولَم يعترف أَبدًا . سوف تكبر يا
ابني ، وتَروي لمن يَرثُون بنادقَهُمْ
سيرةَ الدَّمِ فوقَ الحديدْ . . .

– Why did you leave the horse alone?
– To keep the house company, my son.
Houses die when their inhabitants are gone . . .

Eternity opens its gates from a distance
to the traffic of night. The wolves of the wilderness
howl at a frightened moon. And a father
says to his son: Be strong like your grandfather!
Climb with me the last hill of oaks,
my son, and remember: Here the janissary fell
from the mule of war. So be steadfast with me
and we'll return.

– When, father?
– Tomorrow. Perhaps in two days, my son!

A reckless tomorrow chewed at the wind
behind them through the long nights of winter.
The soldiers of Yehoshua ben Nun built
their citadel from the stones of their house. Out of breath
on the path to Qana: Here
Jesus passed one day. Here
he turned water into wine and said
many things about love. My son, remember
tomorrow. Remember crusader citadels
gnawed at by April weeds after
the soldiers' departure . . .

- لماذا تركتَ الحصانَ وحيدًا؟
- لكي يُؤنسَ البيتَ ، يا ولدي ،
فالبيوتُ تموتُ إذا غابَ سُكَّانُها . . .

تفتحُ الأبديَّةُ أبوابَها ، من بعيد ،
لسيَّارة الليل . تعوي ذئابُ
البراري على قَمَر خائف . ويقولُ
أبٌ لابنه : كُنْ قويًّا كجدِّك!
وأصعَدْ معي تلَّةَ السِّنديان الأَخيرةَ
يا ابني ، تذكَّرْ : هُنا وقع الإنكشاريُّ
عَن بَغْلَة الحرب ، فاصمُدْ معي
لنعودْ

- متى يا أبي؟
- غَدًا . ربّما بَعد يومين يا ابني!

وكان غَدٌ طائشٌ يمضغُ الرّيح
خلفهما في ليالي الشِّتاء الطويلةْ .
وكان جنودُ يُهوشْعَ بن نونٍ يبنون
قَلْعَتَهُمْ من حجارة بيتهما . وهما
يلهثان على درب «قانا» : هُنا
مرَّ سيِّدُنا ذاتَ يوم . هُنا
جَعَلَ الماءَ خمرًا . وقالَ كلامًا
كثيرًا عن الحُبّ ، يا ابني تذكر
غدًا . وتذكَّرْ قلاعًا صليبيَّةً
قَضَمَتْها حشائش نيسان بعد
رحيل الجنودْ . . .

How Many Times Will it be Over . . .

He reflects on his days in cigarette smoke
He looks at his pocket watch:
If I could, I would slow down its ticks
to delay the barley's ripening!
He leaves himself, without thinking, worn out:
The time of the harvest has come
The ears of grain are heavy, the sickles abandoned. The country
recedes, now, from its prophetic gate.
The Lebanon summer tells me of my grapes in the south
It tells me of metaphysics.
But my path to God begins
from a star in the south . . .

– Are you speaking to me, father?
– They signed a truce on the island of Rhodes,
my son!
– What about us, what about us, father?
– It's over . . .
– How many times will it be over, father?
– It's over. They did their duty:
They fought the enemy's airplanes with broken guns.
We did our duty. We drew away from the chinaberry tree
so we wouldn't tip the commander's hat.
We sold our wives' rings so they could hunt birds,
my son!

أكَم مَرَّة ينتهي أمرُنا . . .

يتأمَّلُ أيَّامَهُ في دُخان السجائر ،
ينظرُ في ساعة الجَيْب :
لو أستطيع لأبطأتُ دَقَّاتها
كَي أؤخِّرَ نُضْجَ الشَّعير! . . .
ويخرجُ من ذاته مرهقًا نزقًا :
جاءَ وقتُ الحَصادْ
السَّنابلُ مثقلة ، والمناجلُ مُهملةٌ ، والبلادْ
تَبْعُدُ الآنَ عن بابها النبويِّ .
يُحدِّثُني صَيفُ لبنانَ عَن عِنَبي في الجنوب
يُحدِّثُني صَيفُ لبنانَ عمَّا وراء الطبيعةِ
لكنَّ دربي إلى اللهِ يبدأ
من نَجْمَةٍ في الجنوب . . .

– هل تُكلِّمُني يا أبي؟
– عَقدوا هُدْنةً في جزيرةِ رودوس ،
يا ابني!
– وما شأننا نحن ، ما شأننا يا أبي؟
– وانتهى الأمرُ . . .
– كَم مرَّةً ينتهي أمرُنا يا أبي؟
– إنتهى الأمر . قامُوا بواجبهم :
حارَبوا ببنادق مكسورة طائرات العُدوّ .
وقُمنا بواجبنا ، وابتعدنا عن الزَّنْزَلَخْت
لئلّا نُحرِّكَ قُبَّعَةَ القائد العسكريَّ .
وبعنا خواتمَ زوجاتِنا لِيَصيدوا العصافير
يا ولدي!

– Will we remain here, then, father
under the willow of the wind
between the sky and the sea?

– My son! Everything here
will look like something there
We'll look like ourselves at night
The star of eternal likeness will consume us,
my son!

– Father, go easy on me with your words!
– I left the windows open
to the coo of pigeons
I left my face at the edge of the well
I left my words
on their rope strung over the closet
speaking. I left the darkness
to its night wrapped with the wool of my waiting
I left the clouds
spreading their garments over fig trees
I left the dream
renewing itself in itself
I left peace
alone, there, on the earth . . .

– Were you dreaming, father, while I was awake?
– Get up, my son. We're going back!

- هَل سنبقى ، إذًا ، ههُنا يا أَبي
تحتَ صفصافة الرَّيح
بين السَّموات والبحر؟

- يا ولدي! كُلُّ شيء هُنا
سوفَ يُشبهُ شيئًا هُناك
سنُشْبهُ أَنفُسَنا في اللَّيالي
ستحرقُنا نجمة الشَّبَه السرمديَّةُ
يا وَلدي!

- يا أَبي ، خفِّف القولَ عنِّي!
- تركتُ النوافذَ مفتوحةً
لهديل الحَمامْ
تركتُ على حافَّة البئر وجهي
تركتُ الكلامْ
على حَبْله فوقَ حبل الخزانة
يحكي ، تركتُ الظَّلامْ
على ليله يتدثَّرُ صُوفَ انتظاري
تركتُ الغمامْ
على شجر التّين ينشر سِرْوالَهُ
وتركتُ المَنامْ
يُجدِّدُ في ذاته ذاتَهُ
وتركتُ السَّلام
وحيدًا ، هناك على الأَرض . . .

- هل كُنتَ تحلُمُ في يَقْظتي يا أَبي؟
- قُمْ . سَنَرْجِعُ يا وَلدي!

To My End and to Its End . . .

– Are you tired of walking
my son, are you getting tired?
– Yes, father.
Your night has grown long on the road
and your heart has flowed over your night's earth
– You're still as lithe as a cat
so climb up on my shoulders
In a little while we'll cross
the forest of terebinth and oak
This is the northern Galilee
Lebanon is behind us
The sky is ours, all of it, from Damascus
to the beautiful wall of Acre
– And then what?
– We'll return to the house
Do you know the way, my son?
– Yes, father:
East of the carob tree on the main street there's
a small path crowded by cactus
at its opening. Then it leads, wider and wider,
to the well where it looks out
on the orchard of my uncle Jamil
who sells tobacco and sweets
Then it gets lost on a threshing floor before

إلى آخِري وإلى آخِره . . .

- هَل تَعِبْتَ من المَشي
يا وَلَدي ، هل تَعِبْتْ؟
- نَعَم ، يا أبي
طالَ ليلُكَ في الدَّرب ،
والقلبُ سالَ على أرضٍ لَيْلِكَ
- ما زِلْتَ في خِفّة القطّ
فاصْعَدْ إلى كتفيَّ ،
سنقطعُ عمّا قليلْ
غابةَ البُطْم والسَّنديان الأخيرة
هذا شمالُ الجليلْ
ولبنانُ من خلفنا ،
والسماءُ لنا كُلُّها من دمشقَ
إلى سورِ عكّا الجميلْ
- ثمَّ ماذا؟
- نعودُ إلى البيت
هل تعرف الدَّربَ يا ابني
- نَعم ، يا أبي :
شرقَ خرّوبَة الشارعِ العامِّ
دربٌ صغيرٌ يضيقُ بصبّاره
في البدايَة ، ثمّ يسيرُ إلى البئر
أوْسَعَ أوْسَعَ ، ثمَّ يُطِلُّ
على كَرْمِ عمّي «جميلْ»
بائع التّبغِ والحَلويّات ،
ثمَّ يضيعُ على بَيْدَرٍ قبل

[37]

it straightens out and settles in at home
in the shape of a parrot
– Do you know the house, my son?
– I know it like I know the path:
Jasmine winds around an iron gate
Footprints of light on the stone stairs
Sunflowers stare at what lies behind the place
Friendly bees prepare breakfast for my grandfather
on a reed tray
In the yard there's a well and a willow tree and a horse
Behind the fence, a tomorrow, thumbing through our papers . . .

– Oh father, are you getting tired?
Do I see sweat in your eyes?
– My son, I am tired . . . Can you carry me?
– Like you used to carry me, father
I'll carry this longing
for
my beginning
and its beginning
I'll follow this road to
my end . . . and to its end!

أَن يستقيمَ ويَجلس في البيت ،

في شكل بَبْغَاءَ ،

– هل تعرف البيتَ ، يا ولدي؟

– مثلما أَعرف الدربَ أَعرفُهُ :

ياسمينٌ يُطوِّقُ بوّابةً من حديدْ

ودعساتُ ضوءٍ على الدرج الحجريِّ

وعبّادُ شمسٍ يُحَدِّقُ في ما وراء المكان

ونحلٌ أَليفٌ يُعدُّ الفطور لجدِّي

على طبق الخيزران ،

وفي باحة البيت بئرٌ وصفصافةٌ وحصانْ

وخلفَ السياج غدٌ يتصفَّحُ أَوراقنا . . .

– يا أَبي ، هل تَعِبْت

أَرى عرقًا في عيونك؟

– يا ابني تعبتُ . . . أَتحملُني؟

– مثلما كنتَ تحملني يا أَبي ،

وسأحمل هذا الحنين

إلى

أَوَّلي وإلى أَوَّلهْ

وسأقطعُ هذا الطريق إلى

آخري . . وإلى آخرهِ!

II.

Abel's Space

فضاءُ هابيل

Ismael's *'Oud*

A mare dances on two strings – that's how
Ismael's fingers listen to his blood. The villages scatter
like poppies in the rhythm. There's neither
night there nor day. Divine *tarab*
touches us. All points rush towards
the elemental
Hallelujah
Hallelujah
Everything will begin anew

He owns the old *'oud*, our neighbor
in the oak forest. He carries his time disguised
in the clothes of a singing madman. The war had ended
and the ashes of our village disappeared in a black cloud on which
the phoenix had not yet been born, as
we'd expected. The night's blood had not dried on
the shirts of our dead. Plants hadn't grown,
as forgetfulness had expected,
in the soldiers' helmets
Hallelujah
Hallelujah
Everything will begin anew

عُودُ إسماعيل

فَرَسٌ على وَتَرَيْن ترقُصُ – هكذا
تُصْغي أصابعُهُ إلى دَمه ، وتنتشرُ القُرى
كشقائق النعمان في الإيقاع . لا
لَيْلَ هُناك ولا نهارٌ . مَسَّنا
طربٌ سَماويٌّ ، وهَرْوَلَت الجهاتُ إلى
الهيولى
هَلِّلويا ،
هَلِّلويا ،
كُلُّ شيءٍ سوفَ يبدأ من جديدِ

هُوَ صاحبُ العُود القديمِ ، وجارُنا
في غابة البَلُّوط . يحملُ وقتَهُ مُتَخَفِّيًا
في زِيِّ مَجنونٍ يُغَنِّي . كانت الحربُ انتهتْ
ورمادُ قريتنا اختفى بسحابة سوداءَ لَم
يُولَدْ عليها طائرُ الفينيق بَعْدُ ، كما
تَوَقَّعْنا ، ولم تَنْشَفْ دماءُ اللّيل في
قُمْصان موتانا . ولَم تطلعْ نباتاتٌ ، كما
يَتَوَقَّعُ النسيانُ ،في خُوَذ الجنود
هَلِّلويا
هَلِّلويا ،
كُلُّ شيءٍ سوف يبدأ من جديدِ

Like the remains of the desert, space recedes from time
a distance that allows the poem to explode. Ismael
descends to us, at night, and sings: Oh stranger
I am the stranger, and you are from me, oh stranger! The desert
departs in his words. His words disregard the force
of things: Oh *'oud* . . . bring back what's been lost and sacrifice me
upon it. From one distance to another
Hallelujah
Hallelujah
Everything will begin anew

Meaning displaces us . . . so we fly from the foot of one marble mountain
to another. And we run between two blue abysses
Our dreams do not awaken, nor do the guards of the place
leave the space of Ismael. There's neither earth there
nor sky. A collective *tarab* touches us, before
the two-string isthmus. Sing for us, Ismael
so that everything will become possible, near existence
Hallelujah
Hallelujah
Everything will begin anew

In Ismael's *'oud* the Sumerian wedding rises up
to the ends of the sword. There's neither existence there
nor nothingness. A lust for creation touches us:

كَبَقِيَّةِ الصَّحراء ، يَنْحَسِرُ الفَضاءُ عَن الزّمان
مسافةً تَكفي لِتَنفجرَ القصيدةُ . كان إسماعيلُ
يَهبطُ بيننا ، لَيلًا ، ويُنشِدُ : يا غريبُ ،
أَنا الغَريبُ ، وأَنتَ مِنّي يا غريبُ! فَترحَلُ
الصحراءُ في الكلماتِ . والكلماتُ تُهمِلُ قُوَّةَ
الأشياء : عُدْ يا عُوُدُ . . بالمفقودِ ، واذبَحْني
عَلَيْهِ ، من البَعيدِ إلى البَعيدِ
هَلِّلُويا
هَلِّلُويا ،
كُلُّ شيءٍ سوف يبدأ من جديد

يتحرَّكُ المَعنى بِنا . . فَنطيرُ من سَفْحٍ إلى
سَفحٍ رُخاميٍّ . ونركُضُ بين هاوِيَتَيْنِ زُرْقاوينِ .
لا أَحلامُنا تصحو ، ولا حَرَسُ المَكان
يُغادرونَ فضاءَ إسماعيلَ . لا أَرضَ هُناكَ
ولا سماءٌ . مَسَّنا طربٌ جَماعيٌّ أمامَ
البَرْزَخ المصنوع مِنْ وَتَرَيْن . إسماعيلُ . . . غَنِّ
لنا ، لِيصبح كُلُّ شيءٍ مُّمكنًا قُرْبَ الوجودِ
هَلِّلُويا
هَلِّلُويا ،
كُلُّ شيءٍ سوفَ يبدأ من جديد

في عُودِ إسماعيلَ يرتفعُ الزَّفافُ السُّومَريُّ
إلى أَقاصي السَّيْفِ . لا عَدَمٌ هُناك
ولا وجودٌ . مَسَّنا شَبَقٌ إلى التَّكْوينِ :

From one string water flows. From two strings flame
ignites. From three, woman / being / revelation
radiate. Sing, Ismael, to meaning, and a bird will hover
over Athens between two histories at sunset . . .
Sing a requiem on a feast day!
Hallelujah
Hallelujah
Everything will begin anew

Beneath the poem: The foreign horses pass. Carts
pass over the prisoners' shoulders. Forgetfulness and Hyksos
pass beneath them. The masters of time
and the philosophers and Imru' al-Qays, mourning a tomorrow
tossed upon the gates of Caesar, pass. They all pass beneath
the poem. The contemporary past, like Tamurlane, passes
beneath it. The prophets pass there also
and listen to the voice of Ismael singing: Oh stranger,
I am the stranger, and you are like me, oh out-of-place stranger
Oh 'oud . . . bring back what's been lost and sacrifice me upon you
From one vein to another
Hallelujah
Hallelujah
Everything will begin anew

من وَتَر يسيلُ الماءُ . من وَتَرين يندلعُ
اللّهيبُ . ومِن ثَلاثَتِهِمْ تَشعُّ المرأةُ/ الكونُ/
التجلّي . غَنِّ إسماعيلُ للمَعْنى يُحَلِّقُ طائرٌ
عندَ الغُروب على أثينا بين تاريخين . . .
غَنِّ جنازةً في يوم عيد!
هَلِّلويا
هَلِّلويا ،
كُلُّ شيءٍ سوف يبدأ من جَديد

تَحْتَ القصيدة : تعبُرُ الخيلُ الغريبةُ . تعبُرُ
العرباتُ فوق كواهلِ الأَسَرى . ويعبُرُ تحتها
النسيانُ والهكسوسُ . يعبُرُ سادةُ الوقت ،
الفلاسفةُ ، امرؤُ القيس الحزينُ على غَد
مُلْقًى على أبواب قيصَرَ . يعبرون جميعُهُمْ تحت
القصيدة . يعبُرُ الماضي المُعاصِرُ مثل تَيْمُورْلُنْك
يعبُرُ تحتها . والأنبياءُ هناك يعبرون
ويُنْصتون لصوت إسماعيل يُنشدُ : يا غَريبُ ،
أنا الغريبُ ، وأنتَ مثلي يا غريبَ الدّار ،
عُدْ . . . يا عُودُ بالمفقودِ ، واذبَحْني عَلَيْكَ
من الوريدِ إلى الوريدِ
هَلِّلويا
هَلِّلويا ،
كُلُّ شيءٍ سوف يبدأ من جديدِ

Strangers' Walk

I know the house from the bunch of sage. The first of the
windows leans toward the butterflies . . . blue . . .
red. I know the clouds' handwriting and the well where
it will wait for the village women in summer. I know
what the dove says when it lays an egg on the mouth of
a gun. I know who opens the door to the jasmine
as it opens our dreams to the evening guests . . .

The strangers' carriage still hasn't arrived

No one's arrived. Leave me there like
you'd leave your greeting at the entrance of a house. To me or
to someone else, without concern for who'll hear it
first. Leave me, there, a few words for myself:
Was I alone? "Solitary, like the soul in
a body," when you said, once: I love you both,
you and the water. The water shone in everything,
like a guitar that let itself cry!

The strangers' guitar still hasn't arrived

نُزْهَةُ الغُرَباء

أَعرفُ البَيْتَ من خُصْلَة المَزْمِيَّة . أُولى
النوافذ تَجنحُ نحوَ الفراشات . . . زرقاءَ . . .
حمراءَ . أَعرفُ خطَّ السحاب وفي أَيِّ
بئر سَيَنْتَظِرُ القَرَويَّات في الصَّيف . أَعرفُ
ماذا تقولُ الحمامةُ حين تبيضُ على فُوَّهَة
البُندقِيَّة . أَعرفُ مَنْ يفتح البابَ للياسمينة
وهي تُفتِّح أَحلامَنا لضيوف المساءْ . . .

لم تَصلْ بعد مَرْكَبَةُ الغُرباءْ

لم يَصلْ أَحَدٌ . فاتْرُكيني هُناك كما
تتركين التحيَّةَ في مدخل البيت . ليْ أو
لغَيري ، ولا تحفلين بمَن سوف يسمعُها
أَوَّلاً . واتركيني هُناك كلامًا لنفسيَ :
هَل كنتُ وحدي «وحيدًا كما الرُّوحُ في
جَسَد»؟ عندما قلت يومًا : أُحبُّكُما ،
أَنتَ والماء . فالتمعَ الماءُ في كلِّ شيء ،
كجيتارةٍ تركَت نفسَها للبُكاءْ!

لم تَصلْ بعد جيتارة الغُرَباءْ

Let's be good! Take me to the sea at
sunset, so I'll hear what it tells you
when it returns to itself, still, still.
I won't change. I'll slip into a wave
and say: Take me to the sea again. This is what
the frightened do with themselves: They go to
the sea when a star, aflame in the sky, torments them

The strangers' song still hasn't arrived

I know the house from the fluttering scarves. The first of the
doves cries on my shoulders. Beneath the sky
of the Gospels a child runs aimlessly. Water
runs. The pines run. The wind runs in
the wind. The earth runs in itself. I said:
don't rush to leave the house . . . Nothing
prevents this place from pausing for a moment,
here, while you put on the day's shirt and
the shoes of the wind

The strangers' myth still hasn't arrived . . .

فلنَكُنْ طيّبين! خُذيني إلى البَحر عند
الغروب ، لأسمعَ ماذا يقولُ لك البحرُ
حينَ يعودُ إلى نفسه هادئًا هادئًا .
لن أُغيِّر ما بي . سأندسُّ في مَوْجَة
وأقول : خُذيني إلى البَحر ثانيةً . هكذا
يفعلُ الخائفونَ بأنفسهمْ : يذهبونَ إلى
البحر حين تعذّبهم نجمةٌ أَحْرَقَتْ نفسها في السماءْ

لم تَصِلْ بعد أُغنيةُ الغُرباءْ

أعرفُ البيتَ من خَفقان المناديل . أُولى
الحماماتِ تبكي على كتفيَّ . وتحت سماء
الأناجيل يركضُ طفلٌ بلا سَبَب . يَرْكُضُ
الماءُ ، والسرورُ يركضُ ، والريحُ تركُضُ في
الريح ، والأرضُ تركُضُ في نفسها . قلتُ :
لا تُسرعي في الخروج من البيت . . . لا
شيءَ يمنعُ هذا المكانَ من الانتظار قليلاً
هُنا ، ريثما ترتدينَ قميصَ النَّهار ، وتنتعلينَ
حذاءَ الهواءْ

لم تَصِلْ بعد أُسطورَةُ الغُرباءْ . . .

No one's arrived. So leave me there like
you leave the myth with whomever sees you, and he cries,
and runs in himself afraid of his happiness:
How much I love you. How much you are yourself! Afraid of
his soul: There is no I, now, but she, in me, now
There is no she but I, fragile. How I fear
for my dream to dream of someone other than her
at the end of this song . . .

No one's arrived
Perhaps the strangers lost their way
to the strangers' walk!

لَم يَصِلْ أَحَدٌ . فاتركيني هُناك كما
تتركينَ الخُرافَةَ في أيِّ شخصٍ يراكِ ، فيبكي
ويركضُ في نفسه خائفًا من سعادته :
كم أُحبُّك ، كم أَنت أنت! ومِنْ رُوحِه
خائفًا : لا أَنا الآن إلاّ هيَ الآن في .
ولا هيَ إلاَّ أَنا في هَشاشتِها . كَم أخافُ
على حُلُمي أَن يَرَى حُلُمًا غيرَها في
نهايَةِ هذا الغناءْ . . .

لم يصِل أَحَدٌ
ربّما أَخطأَ الغُرباءُ الطريقَ
إلى نُزهةِ الغُرباءْ!

The Raven's Ink

You find solitude in the desolate carob tree, oh
dark-voiced bell of sunset! What
do they demand of you now? You searched in
Adam's garden, so that a casual killer could conceal his brother
You locked yourself in your blackness
when the victim opened onto his expanse
You went about your business like absence
went about its own. Be alert.
Our resurrection will be deferred, oh raven!

No night is enough for us to dream twice. There is a single
door to our sky. From where will our end come?
We are the descendants of the beginning. We see nothing
but the beginning. So unite with your night's wind, a soothsayer
preaching to emptiness the eternal echo left
by human emptiness around you . . .
You're accused of what's in us. This is the first
blood of our lineage before you. Get out
of Cain's new home
like a mirage flees
from your feathers' ink, oh raven

I find solitude in the night of your voice . . . Absence

حِبْرُ الغُراب

لَكَ خَلْوةٌ في وَحْشة الخُرُوب ، يا
جَرَسَ الغُروب الدّاكنَ الأَصوات! ماذا
يطلبونَ الآنَ منكَ؟ بَحثت في
بُستان آدَم ، كي يواري قاتلٌ ضَجرٌ أخاهُ ،
وانغلفتَ على سوادكَ
عندما انفَتَحَ القتيلُ على مَداهُ ،
وانصرَفْتَ إلى شُؤونك مثلما انصرفَ الغِيابُ
إلى مشاغله الكَثيرة . فلْتَكُنْ
يَقِظًا . قيامَتُنا سَتُرْجَأُ يا غُراب!

لا لَيْلَ يكفينا لنحلُمَ مَرَّتَين . هُناكَ بابٌ
واحدٌ لسمائنا . من أَينَ تأتينا النهايةُ؟
نحن أحفادَ البدايَة . لا نَرَى
غَيْرَ البدايَة ، فاتْحُدْ بِمهبِّ لَيْلِكَ كاهنًا
يَعِظُ الفَراغَ بما يُخَلِّفُهُ الفراغُ الآدَميُّ
من الصدى الأَبَديِّ حولكَ . . .
أَنْتَ مُتَّهَمٌ بما فينا . وهذا أَوَّلُ
الدَم من سُلالَتنا أمامَكَ ، فابتعِدْ
عن دار قابيلَ الجديدة
مثلما ابتعَدَ السرابُ
عن حِبْرِ ريشَكَ يا غُرابُ

pulls me as I run between the shadows
So I pull the bull's horn. The unknown pushes me, I push it
It lifts me, I lift it toward the ghost suspended like
a ripe eggplant. Is it you, then? So what
do they demand from us now, after stealing my words
from yours and falling asleep on their feet, spears in hand,
in my dream. I wasn't a ghost for them to trace
my steps upon my steps. Be my second brother
I am Abel. Earth brings me back
as a carob tree, for you to sit upon my branch, oh raven

I am you in words. A single book
joins us. I carry the ashes you carry. In the
shade we were only two witnesses, two victims
Two
short
poems
about nature
waiting for destruction to finish its feast

The *Qur'an* illuminates you:
"Then God sent forth a raven, scratching into the earth,
to show him how he might conceal his brother's corpse. He said:
Woe is me! Am I unable to be like this raven?"

لِيَ خَلْوَةٌ في ليل صوتكَ . . . لي غيابُ
راكضٌ بين الظِّلال يشدُّني
فأشدُّ قَرْنَ الثَّور . كان الغَيْبُ يدفعُني وأدفعُه
ويرفعُني وأرفعُه إلى الشَّبَح المُعَلَّق مثل
باذنجانة نَضَجَتْ . أأنْتَ إذاً؟ فماذا
يطلبون الآن منّا بعدما سَرقوا كلامي من
كلامكَ ، ثمَّ ناموا في مَنامي واقفينَ
على الرِّماح . ولم أكُنْ شَبَحًا لكي يمشوا
خُطايَ على خُطايَ . فكُنْ أخي الثَّاني ،
أنا هابيلُ ، يُرْجِعُني التُّرابُ
إليك خَرُّوبًا لتجلسَ فوق غُصني يا غُرابْ

أنا أنتَ في الكلمات . يجمعُنا كتابُ
واحدٌ . لمْ ما عَلَيْكَ من الرَّماد ، ولم
نَكُنْ في الظَّلِّ إلّا شاهدَيْن ضحيَّتَيْن
قصيدتَين
قصيرتَين
عن الطَّبيعة ، ريثما يُنْهي وليمَتَه الخرابْ

ويضيئكَ القرآنُ :
«فَبَعَثَ اللهُ غُرابًا يبحثُ في الأرض
لِيُرِيَهُ كيف يُواري سوءة أخيه ، قال :

The *Qur'an* illuminates you.
Search for our resurrection, and hover, oh raven!

يا وَيلتي أَعجزت أَن أَكونَ مثلَ هذا الغُراب»
ويضيئك القُرآنُ ،
فابحثْ عن قيامَتِنا ، وحَلِّقْ يا غُرَابُ!

The Tatar's Swallows

My horses set the bounds of the sky. I dreamt of
what would come in the afternoon. The Tatars
march beneath me and beneath the sky. They don't dream
of anything beyond the tents they pitch. They don't know
the fate of our goats with the approaching winter wind.
My horses set the bounds of the evening. The Tatars
sneak their names onto the roofs of the villages like swallows
They sleep, peacefully, amidst our grain stalks
They don't dream of what will come in the afternoon when
the sky returns, piece by piece
to its people in the evening

We have a single dream: for the wind to pass,
a friend, and spread the scent of Arabic coffee
over the hills that surround summer and the strangers . . .

I am my dream. Whenever the earth narrows, I expand it
with the wing of a swallow. I expand. I am my dream . . .
And in the crowd I am full of mirrors of myself and questions
about the planets tracing my beloved's footsteps . . .
In my solitude there are paths of pilgrims to Jerusalem –
words plucked out like feathers over stone

سُنونو التتار

على قَدْرِ خَيْلِي تكونُ السَّماءُ . حَلُمْتُ
بما سوف يحدثُ بعدَ الظهيرة . كان التتار
يسيرون تحتي وتحتَ السَّماء ، ولا يحلمون
بشيء وراء الخيام التي نصبوها . ولا يَعرفون
مصائرَ ماعزِنا في مهبِّ الشّتاء القريب .
على قدرِ خَيْلِي يكونُ المساء . وكان التتار
يَدُسُّون أسماءَهُمْ في سقوفِ القُرى كالسُنونو ،
وكانوا ينامونَ بينَ سنابلِنا آمنين ،
ولا يحلمون بما سوف يحدثُ بعد الظهيرة ، حين
تعودُ السماءُ ، رُوَيْدًا رُوَيْدًا ،
إلى أهلِها في المساءْ

لنا حُلُمٌ واحدٌ : أَن يمرَّ الهواءْ
صديقًا ، وينشُرَ رائحةَ القهوةِ العربيّة
فوقَ التّلالِ المُحيطةِ بالصّيف والغرباءْ . . .

أنا حُلُمي . كُلَّما ضاقت الأرضُ وسَّعْتُها
بجناحِ سُنُوّةٍ واتسعْتُ . أنا حُلُمي . . .
في الزّحامِ امتلأتُ بمرآةِ نفسي وأسئلَتي
عن كواكبَ تمشي على قَدَمَيْ مَنْ أحبُّ . . .
وفي عُزلَتي طُرُقٌ للحجيجِ إلى أورشليم –
الكلامُ المُنَتَّفُ كالرّيشِ فوقَ الحجارة ،

How many prophets does the city need to preserve its father's
name and regret: "I fell without a fight?"
How many skies, in every people, must a city leave behind
for it to love its own crimson shawl? Oh dream . . .
don't stare at us like that!
Don't be the last martyr!

I fear for my dream because of the clarity of the butterfly
and the mulberry stains over the horse's neighing
I fear for my dream, because of the father, the son, and those who
pass along the shore of the Mediterranean in search of gods
and the gold of those who came before
I fear for my dream because of my hands
and a star perched
upon my shoulders waiting to sing

We, the people of the ancient nights, have our customs
rising to the moon of the rhyme
We believe our dreams and deny our days
for since the Tatars came, all of our days haven't been our own
Here they are, preparing themselves to leave
forgetting our days behind them. We'll descend, in a little while
to our years in the fields. We'll make our flags from
white sheets. If there must be a flag,

كَمْ مِنْ نَبيٍّ تريدُ المدينةُ كَي تحفظ اسم
أبيها وتندم : «من غير حرب سَقَطْتُ»؟
وكم من سماء تُبَدِّل ، في كَلّ شَعْب ،
ليُعجبها شالُها القرمزيُّ؟ فيَا حُلْميَ . . .
لا تُحَدِّقْ بنا هكذا!
لا تَكُنْ آخِرَ الشُّهَداء!

أخافُ على حُلُمي من وضوح الفراشَةْ
ومن بُقَع التُّوت فوق صهيل الحصان
أخافُ عَلَيْه مِنَ الأَب والابن والعابرينْ
على ساحل الأَبيض المتوسِّط بحثًا عن الآلهَة
وعن ذهَب السَّابقين ،
أخافُ على حُلُمي من يديَّ
ومن نجمة واقفة
على كتفي في انتظار الغناء

لنا ، نحن أَهْلَ اللّيالي القَديمة ، عاداتُنا
في الصُّعود إلى قَمَر القافية
نُصَدِّقُ أحلامَنا ونُكَذّبُ أيَّامَنا ،
فأَيَّامُنا لم تَكُن كُلُّها معنا منذُ جاءَ التتارُ ،
وها هم يُعِدُّونَ أنفسهم للرحيل
وينسون أَيَّامَنا خَلْفَهُمْ ، وسنهبطُ عمّا قليل
إلى عُمرنا في الحُقُول . ونصنعُ أعلامَنا
من شَراشفَ بيضاءَ . إنْ كانَ لا بُدَّ

let it be this way, bare and
unwrinkled by symbols . . . Let's be calm
so we won't make our dreams fly behind the caravan of strangers

We have a single dream: to find
a dream to carry us
like a star carries the dead!

من عَلِم ، فليكُنْ هكذا عاريًا
من رُمُوزٍ تُجَعِّدُهُ . . . ولنكُنْ هادئين
لئلاّ نُطّيِّر أحلامَنا خلفَ قافلةِ الغُرباء

لنا حُلُمٌ واحد : أَن نَجِدْ
حُلُمًا كانَ يحملُنا
مثلما تحملُ النجمةُ المَيّتين!

The Train Passed

The train rushed past
I was waiting
on the platform for a train that passed
The travelers turned toward
their days . . . and I
am still waiting

The violins cry from a distance
A cloud carries me
from its spaces
and breaks up

Nostalgia for obscure things
pulls away and draws near
Forgetfulness does not pull me away
Memory does not draw me near
a woman who
when touched by a moon
cries: I am the moon!

مَرَّ القِطارُ

مَرَّ القِطارُ سَريعًا ،
كُنْتُ أَنتظِرُ
على الرَّصيف قِطارًا مَرَّ ،
وانصرَفَ المُسافرونَ إلى
أَيَّامِهمْ . . . وأَنا
ما زِلتُ أَنتظِرُ

تَبكي الكمنجاتُ عَن بُعْدٍ ،
فتحملني
سحابةٌ من نواحيها
وتنكسِرُ

كانَ الحنينُ إلى أشياءَ غامضةٍ
يَنْأَى وَيَدْنُو ،
فلا النِّسيانُ يُقْصيني ،
ولا التذكُّرُ يُدنيني
من امرأةٍ
إن مَسَّها قمرٌ
صاحَتْ : أنا القَمَرُ

The train rushed past
My time was not
with me on the platform
The hour was different
What time is it now?
On which day did the break
between yesterday and tomorrow happen?
When the gypsies moved on?

Here I was born and not born
So this train will complete my
stubborn birth
while trees walk around me

Here I was present and not present
I will, on this train, run
into my self that had taken its fill
at a river which had died between its banks
as the young man dies
"If only the young man were stone . . ."

The train rushed past
It passed me by, and I
am like a station. I don't know

مَرَّ القطارُ سَريعًا ،
لم يَكن زَمَني
على الرَّصيف معي ،
فالسَّاعةُ اختلفتْ
ما السَّاعةُ الآن؟
ما اليومُ الذي حَدَثَتْ
فيه القَطيعةُ بينَ الأمسِ والغدِ
لَمّا هاجرَ الغَجَرُ؟

هُنا وُلدتُ ولم أُولَدْ
سيُكْملُ ميلادي الحُرُونَ إذًا
هذا القطارُ
ويمشي حولِيَ الشَجَرُ

هُنا وُجدتُ ولم أُوجَدْ
سأعثُرُ في هذا القطارِ
على نفسي التي امتلأتْ
بضفّتين لنهرٍ ماتَ بينهما
كما يموتُ الفتى
«ليت الفتى حَجَرُ . . .»

مَرَّ القطارُ سَريعًا
مَرَّ بي ، وأَنا
مثلُ المحطَّة ، لا أَدري

[69]

whether I'm seeing people off or greeting them:
Welcome, on my platforms
cafés,
offices,
roses,
telephones,
newspapers,
sandwiches,
music,
and a rhyme
for another poet who comes and waits

The train rushed past
It passed me by, and I
am still waiting

أُودِّعُ أَم أَستقبلُ النَّاسَ :
أهلاً ، فوقَ أرصفَتي

مقهى ،

مكاتبٌ ،

وردٌ

هاتفٌ ،

صُحُفٌ

وسندويشاتٌ ،

وموسيقى ،

وقافيةٌ

لشاعرٍ آخرٍ يأتي وينتظرُ

مَرَّ القطارُ سَريعًا

مَرَّ بي ، وأَنا

ما زلتُ أنتظرُ

III.

Chaos at Resurrection's Gate

فوضَى على بابِ القيامة

The Well

I choose a cloudy day to pass by the old well
Perhaps it's filled with sky. Perhaps it's overflowed meaning and
the shepherd's parables. I'll drink a handful of its water.
And I'll say to the dead that surround it: peace, to you who remain
around the well in the butterfly's water! I'll scrape the yellowhead
from a stone: Peace, little stone! Perhaps we
were the wings of a bird that still pains us. Peace to the
moon, circling around its image that it will never
meet! I say to the cypress tree: Pay attention to what the dust
says to you. Perhaps we were two strings of a violin
at a banquet for azure's guards. Perhaps we were
the two arms of a lover . . .
I was walking opposite my self: be strong,
Double, and lift the past like two horns of a goat
in your hands, and sit near your well. Perhaps the stags
of the valley will glance back to you . . . and the voice,
your voice – stone image of the broken present, will glimmer . . .
I still haven't completed my short visit to forgetfulness . . .
I didn't take all of my heart's instruments with me:
my bell on the pine wind
    my stairs near the sky
        my planets around the roofs
            my hoarseness from the sting of ancient salt . . .
I said to Memory: Peace to the ready talk of the grandmother
Taking us to our white days beneath her slumber . . .

البئر

أختارُ يَومًا غائمًا لأَمُرَّ بالبئر القديمة .
رُبَّما امتلأَتْ سماءً . رُبَّما فاضَتْ عن المعنى وعَنْ
أُمْثُولَة الرّاعي . سأشربُ حفنةً من مائها .
وأقول للموتى حوالَيْها : سلامًا ، أيُّها البَاقونَ
حول البئر في ماء الفراشة! أرفَعُ الطَّيُونَ
عن حَجَر : سلامًا أيّها الحَجَرُ الصّغيرُ! لعلَّنا
كُنَّا جناحَيْ طائرٍ ما زال يوجعُنا . سلامًا
أيّها القمَرُ المحلّقُ حَوْلَ صُورته التي لن يلتقي
أبدًا بها! وأقول للسَّرْوِ : انتبِهْ ممّا يقولُ
لَكَ الغبارُ . لعلَّنا كُنَّا هنا وَتَرَيْ كمان
في وليمة حارساتِ اللازَوَرْدِ . لعلَّنا كُنَّا
ذراعَيْ عاشقٍ . . .
قد كنتُ أمشي حَذْوَ نفسيْ : كُنْ قويًّا
يا قريني ، وارفع الماضي كقرنَيْ ماعز
بيديك ، واجلسْ قُربَ بئرك . رُبَّما التفتَتْ
إليكَ أيائلُ الوادي . . . ولاحَ الصوتُ –
صوتُكَ صورةٌ حجريّةٌ للحاضر المكسور . . .
لم أُكمِل زيارتي القصيرةَ بَعْدُ للنسيان . . .
لم اَخُذْ مَعي أدوات قلبي كُلَّها :
جَرَسي على ريح الصنوبر
سُلَّمي قرب السماء
كواكبي حولَ السطوح
وبُحَّتي من لَسْعة الملحِ القديم . . .
وَقُلْتُ للذكرى : سلامًا يا كلامَ الجَدّة العَفَويّ
يأخُذُنا إلى أَيّامنا البيضاء تحتَ نُعاسِها . . .

[75]

My name rings like an old golden lira at the
well's gate. I hear the ancestors' estrangement between
mim and *waw*, distant, like an arid
valley. And I hide my tender weariness. I know that I'll
return, alive, in a few hours, from the well
in which I found neither Yusuf nor his brothers' fear
of echoes. Be careful! Here is where your mother
laid you down, near the gate of the well, and turned to a talisman . . .
Do what you want. Alone, I did what
I wanted: I grew at night in the story within the sides
of the triangle: Egypt, Syria, and Babylon. Alone,
here, I grew without goddesses of the harvest. [They were
washing pebbles in the forest of olive trees, wet
with dew] . . . I saw that I had fallen
from the caravans' journey upon myself, near a snake
I found no one but my ghost to continue. The earth
threw me outside of its earth as my name rang in my footsteps
like a horseshoe: Come close, oh immortal Gilgamesh . . . so I can
return to you, in your name, from this emptiness!
Be my brother! Come with me so that we can scream into the old
well . . . Perhaps it's filled, like a woman, with sky
Perhaps it's overflowed meaning and what will
come, as I await my birth from my first well!
We'll drink a handful of its water
We'll say to the dead that surround it: Peace
to you who live in the butterflies' water
and to you who are dead, peace!

واسْمِيْ يرنُّ كليرة الذَهَب القديمة عِنْدَ
باب البئر . أسْمَعُ وَحْشَةَ الأَسْلاف بين
الميم والواو السحيقَة مثل واد غير ذي
زرع . وأُخفي تَعبي الوديِّ . أعرفُ أنَّني
سأعودُ حيًّا ، بعدَ ساعات ، من البئرِ التي
لم ألْقَ فيها يوسُفَا أو خَوْفَ إخوته
منَ الأصداء . كُنْ حَذِرًا! هُنا وضعَتْك
أُمُّك قُرب باب البئر ، وانصرَفَتْ إلى تَعْويذة . . .
فاصنعْ بنفسك ما تشاءُ . صَنَعْتُ وحدي ما
أشاءُ : كبرتُ ليلًا في الحكاية بينَ أضلاع
المُثلَّث : مصرَ ، سوريّا ، وبابلَ . هُهنا
وَحدي كبرتُ بلا إلهات الزِّراعة . [كُنَّ
يَغْسِلْنَ الحصى في غابة الزَّيتون . كُنَّ مُبلَّلات
بالنَّدى] . . . ورأيتُ أنِّي قد سقطتُ
عليَّ من سَفَر القوافل ، قرب أفعى . لَم
أجِدْ أحَدًا لأُكْملَهُ سوَى شَبَحي . رَمَتْني
الأرضُ خارجَ أرْضها ، واسمي يَرنُّ على خُطَايَ
كحِذْوة الفَرَس : اقتربْ . . لأعود من هذا
الفراغ إليكَ يا جِلجامش الأبديُّ في اسمكَ! . . .
كُنْ أخي! واذهَبْ مَعي لنصيحَ بالبئر
القديمة . . . ربَّما امتلأَتْ كأنثى بالسماء ،
ورُبَّما فاضَت عن المعنى وعمَّا سوف
يحدُثُ في انتظار ولادتي من بئري الأُولى!
سنشربُ حفنةً من مائها ،
سنقولُ للموتى حواليها : سلامًا
أيُّها الأَحياءُ في ماء الفَراش ،
وأيُّها المَوتى ، سَلامًا!

Like the *Nun* in *Surat al-Rahman*

In the olive grove, east
of the wells my grandfather withdrew into his abandoned
shadow. Mythical grass
didn't grow there
Nor did the lilac's cloud
flow through the scene

The land is like cloth woven
with a needle of sumac in his broken
dream . . . My grandfather woke from his sleep
to gather weeds from his orchard
that had been buried beneath the black asphalt . . .

He taught me the *Qur'an* beneath the sweet basil tree
east of the well
We came from Adam and from Eve
in the heaven of forgetfulness.
Oh grandfather! I'm the last of the living
in the desert. So let's ascend!

The sea and the desert that surround his
bare unguarded name

كالنّون في سورة الرحمن

في غابة الزَّيتون ، شَرْقَ
الينابيع انطَوَى جَدِّي على ظِلِّهِ
المهجور . لم يَنْبُتْ على ظِلِّهِ
عُشْبٌ خُرافيٌّ ،
ولا غيمةُ اللَّيْلَك
سالَتْ داخل المشهَدْ

الأَرضُ مثل الثوب منسوجةٌ
بإبرة السُّمَّاق في حُلْمِه
المكسور . . . جدِّي هَبَّ من نومِهِ
كَي يجمَعَ الأعشابَ من كرمِهِ
المطمور تحتَ الشارع الأسودْ . . .

عَلَّمَني القرآنَ في دوحة الريحان
شَرْقَ البئر ،
من آدم جئنا ومن حوَّاءَ
في جنَّةِ النسيانِ .
يا جدِّي! أنا آخِرُ الأحياء
في الصّحراء ، فلنصعدْ!

البحرُ والصحراءُ حولَ اسمِهِ
العاري من الحُرَّاس

didn't know my grandfather or his children
who stand now around the *nun* in *Surat al-Rahman*
Oh God . . . bear witness!

As for him, born of himself
buried alive, near the fire
in himself
he'll grant the griffin what it needs of
his charred secret after him
to illuminate the temple

In the olive grove, east of the wells
my grandfather withdrew into his abandoned
shadow. No sun rose over it
No shadow fell across it
And my grandfather is, always, further . . .

لم يعرفا جدِّي ولا أَبناءَهُ
الواقفين الآنَ حولَ «النون»
في سورة «الرحمن» ،
اللهم . . . فلتشهَدْ!

أمَّا هُوَ المولود من نفسه
الموءودُ ، قُرب النّار ،
في نفسه ،
فليَمْنَح العنقاءَ من سرِّه
المحروق ما تحتاجُهُ بعده
كي تُشْعِلَ الأضواءَ في المَعْبَد

في غابة الزّيتون ، شَرْقَ الينَابيع
انطوى جدّي على ظلِّه
المهجور . لم تُشْرِق على ظلِّهِ
شمسٌ . ولم يهبط على ظلِّهِ
ظلٌّ ،
وجدِّي دائمًا ، أبعْد . . .

Huriyya's Teachings

I

One day I thought about leaving. A goldfinch landed on
her hand and slept. It was enough to quickly run my hand over the
bars of a trellis . . . for her to realize that my glass of wine
was full. It was enough to go to sleep early for her to see
my dream clearly, to lengthen her night so she could watch over it . . .
It was enough for one of my letters to arrive to know that
my address had changed, at the prison grounds, and that
my days hovered over her . . . and before her

II

My mother counts my fingers and toes from a distance.
She combs me with a braid of her golden hair. She searches
in my underwear for foreign women
and mends my torn socks. She didn't watch me grow up
as we both wanted: she and I. We were separated at the slope of
marble . . . and clouds waved to us and to a goat
that inherits the place. Exile establishes for us two languages:
a spoken one . . . so the pigeons will grasp it and preserve the memory,
and a classical one . . . so I can explain to the shadows their shadows!

تعاليمُ حُوريَّة

I

فَكَّرتُ يومًا بالرّحيل ، فحطَّ حَسُّونٌ على
يَدها ونام . وكان يكفي أن أُداعب غُصْنَ
داليَة على عَجَل . . . لتُدْرِك أنَّ كأسَ نبيذي
امتلأَتْ . ويكفي أن أنام مُبَكِّرًا لتَرَى
منامي واضحًا ، فتطيلُ لَيْلَتها لتحرسَه . . .
ويكفي أن تجيء رسالةٌ منّي لتعرف أنَّ
عنواني تغيَّر ، فوقَ قارعَة السّجون ، وأنَّ
أيّامي تُحوِّمُ حَوْلَها . . . وحِيالَها . . .

II

أُمِّي تَعُدُّ أصابعي العشرينَ عن بُعْد .
تَمَشّطني بخُصْلَة شعرها الذهبيّ . تبحثُ
في ثيابي الداخليَّة عن نساء أجنبيَّات ،
وَتَرْفُو جَوْرَبي المَقطوعَ . لَم أكبَرْ على يَدها
كما شئنا : أنا وَهيَ ، إفترقنا عندَ مُنْحدَر
الرُّخام . . . ولوَّحت سُحُبٌ لنا ، ولِماعز
يَرِثُ المَكانَ . وأنْشَأَ المَنفى لنا لغتين :
دارجةً . . . ليفهَمَها الحمامُ ويحفظ الذّكرى
وفُصْحَى . . . كي أُفسِّر للظّلال ظلالَها!

III

I'm still alive in your ocean. You didn't tell me what
a mother tells her sick son. I fell ill from the copper
moon on the Bedouin's tent. Do you remember
the road of our exile to Lebanon, where you forgot me
and the bag of bread? [It was wheat bread.]
I didn't scream so I wouldn't wake the guards. The scent of dew
set me on your shoulders. Oh gazelle who lost
there its shelter and its mate . . .

IV

No time, around you, for sentimental talk.
You blended the whole afternoon with basil. You baked, in sumac,
the crest of the rooster. I know what devastates your heart, pierced
by the peacock, since you were expelled from Eden a second time.
Our whole world has changed. Our voices have changed. Even
our greetings to each other fall without an echo,
like a button from a dress, on the sand. Say: Good morning!
Say anything at all to me, so that life will treat me tenderly.

V

She's Hagar's sister. Her sister through her mother. With flutes
she mourns the dead who haven't died. There are no graves around
her tent to know how the sky will open. She doesn't
see the desert behind my fingers so she'll see her garden

ما زلتُ حيًّا في خضَمِّكِ . لم تَقُولي ما
تقولُ الأُمُّ للوَلَدِ المريض . مَرِضْتُ من قَمَر
النّحاس على خيام البَدْو . هل تتذكَّرين
طريق هجرتنا إلى لَبنانَ ، حَيْثُ نسيتِني
ونسيتِ كِيسَ الخُبْز [كانَ الخبزُ قمحيًّا .]
ولَم أصْرَخْ لئلاَّ أوقظَ الحُرَّاسَ . حَطَّتني
على كتفَيْكِ رائحةُ النَّدى . يا ظَبْيَةً فَقَدَت
هُناكَ كِنَاسَها وغزالها . . .

IV

لا وَقْتَ حَوْلَكِ للكلام العاطفيِّ .
عَجَنْتِ بالحَبَقِ الظهيرةَ كُلَّها . وخَبَزْتِ للسُّمَّاق
عُرْفَ الدِّيك . أعْرِفُ ما يُخَرِّبُ قلبَكِ المَثْقُوبَ
بالطَّاووس ، مُنْذُ طُرِدت ثانيةً من الفردوس .
عالَمُنا تغَيَّر كُلُّهُ ، فتغيَّرتْ أصواتُنا . حتَّى
التحيَّةُ بيننا وقَعَتْ كزرِّ الثَّوْب فوقَ الرَّمل ،
لم تُسمِعْ صدًى . قُولي : صباحَ الخَير!
قولي أيَّ شيء لي لتمنَحَني الحياةُ دَلالَها .

هي أختُ هاجَرَ . أختُها من أُمِّها . تبكي
مع النايات مَوْتى لم يموتوا . لا مقابر حول
خيمتِها لتعرفَ كيف تَنْفَتِحُ السماءُ ، ولا

on the face of the mirage. Ancient time runs
with her to an ineluctable futility: Her father flew, like
a Circassian, on the wedding's horse. And her mother
prepared, without crying, the henna for her husband's wife,
and made sure her anklet was in place . . .

VI

We only meet parting at the crossroads of speech.
She says to me, for example: marry any foreign
woman, prettier than a local, but don't
trust any woman but me. And don't always
trust your memories. Don't burn up in order to light up your mother
That's her beautiful calling. Don't long for appointments
with the dew. Be realistic, like the sky. And drop the nostalgia
for your grandfather's black cloak and for your grandmother's
endless bribes. Burst, like a colt, into the world.
Be yourself wherever you are. Carry
only the burden of your heart . . . And return when
your country opens onto countries, and changes its state . . .

VII

My mother lights up the last stars of Canaan
around my mirror
and throws her shawl into my last poem!

ترى الصحراءَ خلفَ أصابعي لتَرَى حديقَتَها
على وَجه السراب فيركُض الزَّمنُ القديمُ
بها إلى عَبَثٍ ضروريٍّ : أبوها طار مثلَ
الشَّرْكسيِّ على حصان العُرْس . أمَّا أُمُّها
فلقد أعدَّتْ ، دونَ أن تبكي ، لِزَوجة زَوْجها
حِنَّاءَها ، وتفحَّصَتْ خلخالَها . . .

VI

لا نلتقي إلاَّ وداعًا عند مُفْتَرَق الحديث .
تقول لي مثلاً : تزوَّجْ أيَّةَ امرأةٍ مِنَ
الغُرباء ، أجمل من بنات الحيِّ . لكنْ ، لا
تُصدِّقْ أيَّةَ امرأة سِوايَ . ولا تُصدِّقْ
ذكرياتِكَ دائمًا . لا تَحْتَرقْ لتضيءَ أُمَّكَ ،
تلكَ مِهْنَتُها الجميلةُ ، لا تحنّ إلى مواعيد
النَّدى . كُنْ واقعيًّا كالسَّماء . ولا تحنّ
إلى عباءة جدِّكَ السَّوداء ، أو رَشَوَات
جدَّتكَ الكثيرة ، وانطلقْ كالمُهْر في الدَّنيا .
وكُنْ مَنْ أَنت حيث تكون . واحملْ
عبءَ قلبِكَ وَحْدَهُ . . . وارجع إذا
اتَّسعَتْ بلادُكَ للبلاد وغيَّرتْ أحوالَها . . .

VII

أُمِّي تُضيءُ نُجومَ كَنْعَانَ الأَخيرَة ،
حولَ مراثي ،
وتَرمي ، في قصيدتيَ الأَخيرَة ، شالَها!

Ivory Combs

Clouds descended from the citadel, blue
toward the alleys . . .
    A silk shawl flies off
        A flock of doves flies off
On the surface of a puddle of water the sky strolls
a little, then flies off
And my soul, like a worker bee, flies through the alleys
The sea ate away at its bread, the bread of Acre
It's been polishing its ring for five thousand years
and throwing its cheek against its cheek . . .
in the long, long rites of marriage

The poem says:
Let's wait
until the window falls
upon this travel guide

I enter from its stone armpit, like
a wave enters eternity. I cross
ages as if I were crossing rooms
I see in myself the stuff of intimate time:
a mirror of a Canaanite girl

أمشاطٌ عاجيّة

مِنَ القَلْعَة انحدَرَ الغيمُ أزرقَ
نحوَ الأزِقَّة . . .
شالُ الحرير يطيرُ
وسربُ الحمام يطيرُ
وفي بِرْكَة الماء تمشي السماءُ قليلاً
على وَجهها وتطيرُ
ورُوحي تطيرُ ، كعامِلة النَّحْل ، بينَ الأزِقَّة
والبحرُ يأكُلُ من خبزها ، خبز عَكّا
ويفرُكُ خاتَمها مُنْذُ خَمْسَة آلاف عام
ويرمي على خدِّها خَدَّهُ . . .
في طقوسِ الزِّفافِ الطويل الطويلْ

تقولُ القصيدةُ :
فلننتظِرْ
ريثما تسقطُ النافذةْ
فوق «اَلْبُوم» هذا الدَّليل السياحيّ

أدخُلُ من إبْطِها الحجريِّ ، كما
يدخُلُ الموجُ في الأبديَّة . أعبُرُ
بينَ العُصور كأنّي أعبُرُ بين الغُرَف
أرى في محتويات الزَّمان الأليفَة :
مرأَة بِنْتٍ لكنعانَ ،

[89]

an ivory comb
a bowl of Assyrian soup
the sword of the defender of his Persian master's sleep
the sudden leap of falcons from one flag to another
above the masts of the fleets . . .

If I had another present
I would have possessed the keys of my yesterday
If my yesterday were with me
I would have possessed all my tomorrow . . .

Obscure is my journey in the long alley
toward an obscured moon over the copper
market. Here there's a palm tree that bears the tower for me,
and the lingering obsession of a song that moves the simple instruments
of a recurrent tragedy around me. Imagination
is a hungry peddler here, wandering, familiar, over the dust
As if what was to happen to me at Caesar's coming celebrations
had nothing to do with me!

My lover and I drink
water's joy
from a single cloud
and drop in a single stroke
into a single jar!

أمشاطَ شَعْرٍ من العاجِ ،
صَحْنَ الحَسَّاءِ الأشوريَّ ،
سَيْفَ المُدافعِ عن نَوْمِ سَيِّدَه الفارسيِّ ،
وقفزَ الصقورِ المُفاجئَ من عَلَمٍ نحوَ آخَرَ
فوقَ صواري الأساطيلِ . . .

لو كانَ لي حاضرٌ آخرُ
لامتلكتُ مفاتيح أمسي
ولو كان أمسي معي
لامتلكتُ غَدِي كُلَّهُ . . .

غامضٌ سَفَري في الزِّقاقِ الطويلِ
المؤدِّي إلى قَمَرٍ غامضٍ فوقَ سُوقِ
النّحاس . هنا نخلةٌ تحملُ البرجَ عنِّي ،
وهاجَسُ أُغنِيَّةٍ تنقلُ الأدواتِ البسيطةَ
حولي ، لِصُنْعِ تُراجيديا مُكَرَّرة ، والخيالُ
هُنا بائعٌ جائعٌ يتجوَّلُ فوقَ الغبارِ أليفًا ،
كأنَّي لا شأنَ لي بالذي سوف يحدُثُ
لي في احتفالاتِ يوليوسَ قَيْصَرَ . . . عمَّا قليل!

أنا والحَبيبةُ نشربُ
ماءَ المَسَرّةِ
من غيمةٍ واحدةْ
ونهبط في جَرَّةٍ واحدةْ!

[91]

I anchored in her port, for no reason, only
because my mother lost her scarves here . . .
There's no myth for me here. I don't trade
with gods or negotiate with them. There's no myth
for me here to fill my memory with barley
and with the names of its guardians standing on my shoulders
waiting for the Pharaoh's daybreak. There's no sword for me
There's no myth for me here, to divorce my mother who
had me carry her scarves, cloud by cloud, over
the old port of Acre . . . at the hour of departure!

But other things will follow
Henry will deceive
Qalaun. In a little while
the clouds will rise, red, over the rows of palms . . .

رَسَوْتُ بميِنائها ، لا لشيءٍ سوى
أَنَّ أُمّي أضاعَت مناديلها ههُنا . . .
لا خرافةَ لي ههنا . لا أُقايضُ
آلهةً أو أُفاوضُ آلهةً . لا خرافةَ
لي ههُنا كي أُعبّىءَ ذاكِرتي بالشعير
وأسماء حُرّاسها الواقفينَ على كتفيَّ
انتظارًا لفجرٍ تُحتُمُس . لا سيف لي ،
لا خرافة لي هَهنا لأُطلّقَ أُمّي الّتي
حَمَّلْتني مناديلَها ، غيمةً غيمةً ، فوقَ
ميناء عكّا القديمة . . . عندَ الرحيلْ!

ستحدث أشياءُ أُخَرَى ،
سيكذبُ هنري على
قَلاوونَ ، بعدَ قليلْ
سيرتفعُ الغيمُ أحمرَ فوقَ صُفوفِ النّخيلْ . . .

The Phases of Anat

Poetry is our ladder to a moon hung by Anat
over her garden, a mirror for hopeless lovers. She walks
through the wilds of her self two unreconciled women:
One returns water to the source
the other brings fire to the forests
As for the horses
let them dance for a long while over the two abysses
There's neither death there . . . nor life.
My poem is the foam of a gasp and the cry of an animal
on its high ascent
on its bare descent: Anat!
I want you both, together, love and war. Oh Anat
to hell with me . . . I love you, Anat!
Anat kills herself
    in herself
        for herself
And she recreates distance so creatures can pass
before her distant image over Mesopotamia
and over Syria. North, south, east, and west obey
with an azure staff and the virgin's ring: Don't
be late in the underworld. Return
to nature and to human nature, oh Anat!
The well water, after you, has dried up. The basins
and rivers dried up after your death. Tears

أطوار أنات

الشِّعْرُ سُلَّمُنا إلى قَمَرٍ تُعَلِّقُهُ أَناتُ
على حَديقَتِها ، كمرأةٍ لعُشّاقٍ بلا أَمَلٍ ، وتُضي
في بَراري نَفسِها امرأتَينِ لا تتصالَحانِ :
هُنالِكَ امرأةٌ تُعيدُ الماءَ للينبوعِ ،
وامرأةٌ تقودُ النّارَ في الغاباتِ ،
أَمّا الخيلُ
فلترقُصْ طَويلاً فوقَ هاويتَينِ ،
لا مَوْتٌ هُناكَ . . ولا حياةْ .
وقصيدتي زَبَدُ اللُّهاثِ وصرخةُ الحيوانْ
عندَ صُعُودِهِ العالي
وعند هُبُوطِهِ العاريّ : أَناتُ!
أَنا أُريدُكما معًا ، حُبًّا وحَربًا يا أَناتُ
فإلى جَهَنَّمَ بِيْ . . . أُحبُّكِ يا أَناتْ!
وأَناتُ تقتُلُ نَفسَها
في نَفسِها
ولنَفْسِها
وتُعيدُ تكوينَ المسافةِ كي تمرَّ الكائناتُ
أَمامَ صورتِها البعيدةِ فوقَ أَرضِ الرافدينْ
وفوقَ سُوريًا . وتأتَمِرُ الجهاتُ
بصَوْلجانِ اللازَوَرْدِ وخاتَمِ العذراءِ : لا
تتأخَّري في العالمِ السُّفليِّ . عُودي من هُناكَ
إلى الطَّبيعةِ والطّبائعِ يا أَناتُ!
جَفَّتْ مياهُ البئرِ بَعْدَكِ ، جَفَّتِ الأَغوارُ
والأَنهارُ جَفَّتْ بعد موتِكِ . والدُّموع

[95]

evaporated from the clay jar. Air cracked
from the dryness like a piece of wood. We broke like a fence
over your absence. Our desires dried up in us. Our prayers
calcified. Nothing lives after your death. Life
dies like words between two travelers to hell
Oh Anat
don't linger any longer in the underworld! Perhaps
new goddesses will descend upon us in your absence
and we'll be ruled by a mirage. Perhaps cunning shepherds
will find a goddess, near nothingness. The priestesses believe her
You'll return, you'll return the land of truth and allegory,
the land of Canaan – the beginning
the land that opens between your communal breasts
and between your communal thighs, so that the miracles will return
to Jericho
At the gate of the abandoned temple . . . there's
neither life nor death
Chaos at resurrection's gate. There's no tomorrow
coming. There's no past coming to bid farewell
No memories
flying from Babylon over our palm tree, nor a
dream to accompany us as we grow old, so we'll inhabit a star
The star is a button on your dress, oh Anat.
Anat creates herself
    of herself
        for herself
She flies behind the vessels of the Greeks

تَبَخَّرَتْ من جَرَّة الفخّار ، وانكسَرَ الهواءُ
من الجفاف كَقطعة الخشب . إنكسرنا كالسياج
على غيابك . جَفَّتِ الرغباتُ فينا . والصلاةُ
تكلَّسَتْ . لا شيءَ يَحيا بعد موتك . والحياةُ
تَموتُ كالكلمات بينَ مُسافرَيْن إلى الجحيم ،
فيا أَناتُ
لا تمكُثي في العالم السُفليِّ أَكثَرُ! رُبَّما
هَبَطَتْ إلهاتٌ جديداتٌ علينا من غيابك
وامتَثلْنا للسراب . ورُبَّما وَجَدَ الرُّعاةُ
الماكرونَ إلهةً ، قرب الهباء وصدَّقَتْها الكاهناتُ
فلتَرْجِعي ، ولتُرجعي أَرضَ الحقيقة والكناية ،
أَرضَ كَنْعانَ البداية ،
أَرضَ نَهْدَيْك المشاع ،
وأرضَ فَخْذَيْكِ المشاع ، لكي تعودَ المعجزاتُ
إلى أَريحا ،
عندَ باب المَعْبَد المهجور . . . لا
موتٌ هناك ولا حياةُ
فَوْضى على باب القيامَة . لا غَدٌ
يأتي . ولا ماضٍ يجيءُ مُودِّعًا .
لا ذكرياتٌ
تطيرُ من أَنحاء بابلَ فوقَ نخلتَنا ، ولا
حُلُمٌ يُسامرُنا لنسكنَ نجمةً ،
هيَ زِرُّ ثوبك ، يا أَناتُ
وأناتُ تخلقُ نفسَها
من نفسِها
وَلنفسِها
وتطيرُ خَلْفَ مراكب الإغريق ،

under another name
Two women never to be reconciled
As for the horses
they'll dance for a long while over the two abysses. There's
neither death there, nor life
There I'm neither alive nor dead
Nor is Anat
Nor is Anat!

في اسمٍ آخَرَ ،
إمرأتينٍ لَن تتصالَحا أبَدًا . . .
وأمَّا الخيلُ
فلترقُصْ طَويلاً فوقَ هاويتين . لا
موتَّ هُناك ولا حياةٌ
لا أنا أَحيا هُنالك ، أو أموتُ
ولا أَنات ُ
ولا أَنات ُ!

The Death of the Phoenix

In the hymns that we sing, there's a
flute
In the flute that shelters us
fire
In the fire that we feed
a green phoenix
In its elegy I couldn't tell
my ashes from your dust

A cloud of lilac would be enough
to hide
the tent of the fishermen from us. Walk
on water – like Jesus – she said to me:
There is no desert for the memory that I bear for you
Nor enemies, from now on, of the roses
that burst from the ruins of your house!

A ring of water circled the
elevated mountain. Tiberius was
the courtyard of the first Eden
I said: the image of the world is
completed in two green eyes

مَصرعُ العَنقاء

في الأَناشيدِ الّتي نُنشِدُها
نايٌ ،
وفي النّايِ الذي يَسْكُنُنا
نارٌ ،
وفي النّارِ التي نُوقِدُها
عنقاءُ خضراءُ ،
وفي مرثِيَّةِ العنقاء لم أَعرفْ
رمادي من غبارِك

*

غَيمةٌ من لَيْلِكِ تكفي
لتُخْفي
خيمةَ الصيّادِ عنّا . فأَمشِ
فوقَ الماءِ كالسيِّد - قالت لي :
فلا صحراءَ للذكرى التي أحملها عنك
ولا أَعداءَ ، منذ الآن ، للورد
الذي يبزُغُ من أَنقاضِ دارِكْ!

*

كان ماءٌ يُشبهُ الخاتَمَ حول
الجَبَلِ العالي . وكانت طبريّا
ساحةً خلفِيَّةً للجنّةِ الأُولى ،
وقلتُ : اكتملَتْ
صُورةُ العالم في عينين خضراوَين

She said: oh my prince, my prisoner
keep my wine in your jars!

The two strangers who burned up in us
are
the ones who wanted to kill us, a little while ago
are
the ones who'll return to their swords, in a little while
are
the ones who ask: Who are you, you two?
– Two shadows of what we were, here, and two names
for the wheat that grows in the bread of battles

I don't want to return now, as
the Crusaders returned, from myself. I am
all this silence between two: gods
on the one hand
and those who invent their names
on the other
I am the shadow that walks on water
I am the witness and the scene
I am the worshiper and the temple
in the land of my siege and yours

قالتْ : يا أميري وأَسيري
ضَعْ خُموري في جِرارِكْ!

الغريبان اللّذان احْتَرَقا فينا
هُما
مَنْ أرادا قَتْلَنا قبلَ قليلٍ
وَهُما
مَنْ يعودان إلى سَيْفَيْهما بعد قليلٍ
وَهُما
مَنْ يقولان لنا : مَنْ أَنتما؟
ـ نحن ظلّان لَمَّا كُنّا هنا ، واسمان
للقمحِ الّذي ينبتُ في خبزِ المعاركْ

لا أُريدُ العودةَ الآن ، كَما
عادَ الصليبيّونَ منّي ، فأَنا
كُلُّ هذا الصمت بين الجهتين : الآلهة
من جهةْ ،
والذين ابتكَرُوا أَسماءَهم
من جهةٍ أُخرى ،
أنا الظلُّ الذي يَمشي على الماء
أنا الشّاهدُ والمشهَدُ
والعابدُ والمَعْبَدُ
في أَرضٍ حصاري وحصارِكْ

Be my lover, between two wars, against the mirror –
she said – I don't want to return now to
my father's fortress. Take me to your orchards. Bring me back
to your mother. Sprinkle me with basil water. Scatter me
upon the silver cup. Brush me. Hold me captive
in your name. Kill me with love
Marry me. Marry me to the rites of the fields
Teach me to play the flute. Burn me so that I'll be born
like a phoenix from my fire and yours!

A shape like a phoenix would
cry, always,
before falling into the water
near the fisherman's tent . . .

What's the point of my waiting and yours?

كُنْ حبيبي بين حَربين على المرأة –
قالت – لا أُريدُ العودةَ الآنَ إلى
حضْنِ أَبي . . . خُذْني إلى كرمِكَ ، واجمعني
إلى أُمَّكَ ، عَطِّرني بماء الحَبَق ، أنثرني
على آنيةِ الفضَّة ، مَشِّطني ، وأدخلني
إلى سِجْنِ اسمكَ ، اقتُلْني من الحبِّ ،
تزَوَّجْني ، وزَوِّجْني التقاليدَ الزراعيَّةَ ،
دَرِّبني على النَّاي ، واحرقني لكي أُولَدَ
كالعنقاءِ من ناري ونارِك!

كان شيءٌ يُشبهُ العنقاءَ
يبكي دامِيًا ،
قبلَ أن يَسْقُطَ في الماء ،
على مقربة من خَيْمَةِ الصيَّاد . . .

ما نَفْعُ انتظاري وانتظارِكْ؟

IV.

A Room to Talk to Oneself

غرفة للكلام مع النفس

Poetic arrangements

The planets did nothing
except
teach me to read:
I have a language in the sky
and a language on the earth
Who am I? Who am I?

I don't want to reply here
Perhaps a star will fall upon its image
Perhaps the forest of chestnut trees will lift
me toward the galaxy at night
and say: You stay here!

The poem is above. It is able
to teach me what it wants
like how to open a window
or put my household affairs in order
among myths. It is able
to wed me to itself . . . in time

My father is below, carrying a thousand-year-old
olive tree

تدابير شعريّة

لم يكُنْ للكواكب دَوْرٌ ،
سِوَى أَنَها
عَلَّمَتْني القراءَةَ :
لي لُغَةٌ في السماءْ
وعلى الأَرض لي لُغَةٌ
مَنْ أنا؟ مَنْ أنا؟

لا أُريدُ الجوابَ هنا .
رَبما وَقَعَتْ نَجمةٌ فوق صورَتِها
رَبّما ارتفعتْ غابةُ الكستنا
بيَ نَحْوَ المجرَّة ، ليلاً ،
وقالتْ : ستبقى هنا!

أَلقصيدةُ فوق ، وفي وُسْعِها
أَن تُعَلِّمني ما تشاءُ
كأَنْ أَفتح النافذةْ
وأُديرُ تدابيري المنزليَّةَ
بينَ الأَساطير . في وسعها
أَن تزوِّجني نفسها . . . زمنا

وأَبي تحت ، يحملُ زيتونةً
عمرُها أَلفُ عامٍ ،

It's neither eastern
nor western.
Perhaps he'll take a rest from the conquerors,
give my shoulder a squeeze,
gather lilies for me

The poem draws away from me
It enters a port of sailors who love wine
and don't return to the same woman twice
and don't feel nostalgia for anything,
nor sorrow!

I haven't died of love, yet
But a mother who notices the glances of her son
at a carnation fears for the vase, for her wound
Then she weeps to ward off an accident
before it arrives
Then she weeps to pull me back from the perilous path
alive, to be here

The poem is what lies between a between. It is able
to illuminate the night with the breasts of a young woman
It is able to illuminate, with an apple, two bodies
It is able to restore,
with the cry of a gardenia, a homeland!

فلا هِيَ شرقيَّةٌ
ولا هِيَ غربيَّةٌ .
رُبَّما يستريح من الفاتحين ،
ويحنو عليَّ قَليلاً ،
ويجمَعُ لِيْ سوسنا

أَلقصيدةُ تبعد عنِّي ،
وتدخلُ ميناءَ بَحَّارة يعشقونَ النبيذَ
ولا يرجعون إلى امرأة مَرَّتَيْن ،
ولا يَحملون حنينًا إلى أَيِّ شيءٍ
ولا شَجَنا!

لم أَمُتْ بعد حُبًّا
ولكنَّ أُمَّا تَرى نَظَرات ابنها
في القرنفل تَخشى على المزهرية من جرحها ،
ثُمَّ تَبكي لتُبْعِدَ حادثةً
قبل أن تصلَ الحادثةْ
ثم تبكي لتُرْجعني من طريقِ المصائد
حيًّا ، لأحيا هنا

أَلقصيدةُ ما بينَ بين ، وفي وُسْعها
أن تُضيءَ اللَّيالي بنَهْدَيْ فتاة ،
وفي وُسعها أن تُضيءَ بتُفَّاحةٍ جَسَدَيْن ،
وفي وُسعها أن تُعيد ،
بصرخة غاردينيا ، وطنا!

The poem is in my hands. It is able
to arrange the affairs of myths
with the work of hands. But I
when I found the poem, dispossessed my self
and I asked it:
Who am I?
Who am I?

أَلْقصيدةُ بينَ يديَّ ، وفي وسعها

أَن تُدير شؤونَ الأَساطير ،

بالعَمَل اليَدويِّ ، ولكنّني

مذ وَجَدتُ القصيدةَ شرَّدتُ نَفسي

وساءَلتها :

مَن أَنا

مَن أَنا؟

From the Byzantine Odes of Abu Firas al-Hamdani

An echo returning. A wide street in the echo
Steps exchange the rattle of a cough, approach
the door, little by little, and draw
away. Family will visit tomorrow
Their Thursday visit. There's our shadow
in the hallway and our sun in the basket
of fruit. There's a mother scolding our jailer:
Why did you pour out our coffee on
the grass, you criminal? There's salt rising from the sea
There's sea rising from the salt. My cell
grew an inch from the voice of the dove. Fly
to Aleppo, oh dove, fly with my ode
and carry a greeting to my cousin!
An echo in the echo. The echo has its metal staircase, its transparence,
                                                                    its dew

ringing with those who climb to their dawn, and those
who descend to their graves through breaks in the horizon . . .
Take me with you to my language! I said:
what's useful lingers in the words of the ode
which rise, like foam, to the surface of the skin of the drums
And in the echo, my cell opens, a balcony
like the dress of the young woman who accompanied me in vain
to the train window. My father doesn't like you,
she said. My mother does. So beware of tomorrow's Sodom

من روميّات أَبي فِراس الحَمداني

صدًى راجعٌ . شارعٌ واسعٌ في الصَّدى
خُطًى تَتَبادَلُ صَوْتَ السُّعال ، وتَدْنو
منَ الباب ، شَيْئًا فشَيْئًا ، وتَنْأى
عن الباب . ثَمَّةَ أَهلٌ يَزُورُونَنا
غدًا ، في خميس الزِّيارات . ثَمَّةَ ظِلٌّ
لنا في المَمَرِّ . وشمسٌ لنا في سلال
الفواكه . ثَمَّةَ أُمٌّ تُعاتِبُ سجّانَنا :
لماذا أَرَقْتَ على العُشْب قهوتَنا يا
شَقيُّ؟ وثَمَّةَ مِلْحٌ يَهُبُّ منَ البَحر ،
ثَمَّةَ بَحْرٌ يَهُبُّ منَ الملح . زنزانتي
اتَّسَعَتْ سنتيمترًا لصوت الحمامة : طيري
إلى حَلَبَ ، يا حمامةُ ، طيري بُرُومِيَّتي
واحملي لابن عمِّي سلامي!
صدًى
للصدى . للصدى سُلَّمٌ مَعْدَنيٌّ ، شَفافيَّةٌ ، وندى
يعجُّ بمَنْ يَصعَدون إلى فجرهم . . . ومَنْ
ينزلونَ إلى قبرهم من ثُقُوب المَدَى . . .
خُذُوني إلى لُغَتي مَعَكُمْ! قلتُ :
ما ينفعُ النَّاسَ بمكَثُ في كَلِمات القصيد
وأَمَّا الطُّبولُ فتطفو على جِلْدها زَبَدا
وزنزانتي اتَّسَعَتْ ، في الصدى ، شرفةً
كَثَوْب الفتاة التي رافَقَتْني سُدَى
إلى شُرُفات القطار ، وقالتْ : أَبي
لا يُحبُّكَ . أُمِّي تُحبُّك . فاحذَرْ سَدُومَ غدا

Don't wait for me Thursday morning. I don't
like thickness when it hides the movements of meaning
within its walls, and leaves me, a solitary body,
to remember its forest . . . The echo has a room
like my cell: a room to talk to itself
My cell is my image. I haven't found anyone around it
to share my morning coffee with,
not a bench to share my isolation with in the evening, nor a scene
to share my perplexity with to reach the right path
So I'll be what the horses bid during the raids:
a prince
a prisoner
or a corpse!
My cell opened wider, a street or two. This echo
is an echo. To the left and right, I'll leave my walls
a master, like a free ghost leaves itself,
and will walk to Aleppo. Oh dove, fly
with my ode. Carry to my cousin
the dew's greeting!

ولا تَنْتَظِرْني ، صبَاحَ الخميس ، أنا لا
أُحِبُّ الكثافَةَ حين تُخَبِّئُ في سجنها
حَرَكات المَعاني ، وتتركُني جَسَدا
يَتَذكَّرُ غاباته وَحْدَهُ . . . للصدى غُرْفَةٌ
كزنزانتي هذه : غُرْفَةٌ للكلام مع النفس ،
زنزانتي صُورَتي لم أجِدْ حَوْلَها أحَدا
يُشاركُني عُزْلَتي في المساء ، ولا مَشْهَدا
أشارِكُهُ حَيْرتي لِبُلوغ الهُدَى .
فلأكُنْ ما تريدُ لِيَ الخَيْلُ في الغَزَوات :
فإمّا أميرًا
وإمّا أسيرًا
وإمّا الردى!
وزنزانتي اتَّسَعَتْ شارعًا شارعين . وهذا الصدى
صدى ، بارحًا سانحًا ، سوف أخرُجُ من حائطي
كما يخرج الشَّبَحُ الحُرُّ من نفسه سَيِّدا
وأمشي إلى حَلَب . يا حمامةُ طيري
بُروميثي ، واحملي لابن عمِّي
سلامَ الندى!

From One Sky to Another
Dreamers Pass

. . . We abandoned our childhood to the butterfly when we left
a little oil on the steps. But we
forgot to greet our mint around us and forgot
to nod to our tomorrow after us . . .
Were it not for the book of the butterfly, around us
the ink of noon would have been white . . .

Oh butterfly, faithful to yourself, be
as you like, before my nostalgia and after
But if you take me as your wing, my madness will remain
with me, aflame. Oh butterfly, born
of yourself, don't abandon me to the boxes designed for me
by craftsmen . . . Don't abandon me!

Dreamers pass from one sky to another
carrying mirrors of water, an entourage of the butterfly
We're able to be as we must
    From one sky
        to another
            dreamers pass

من سماء إلى أُختها
يعبرُ الحالمون

. . وتَرَكْنا طفولتَنا للفراشة ، حين تَرَكْنا
على الدَرَجات قليلاً من الزيت ، لكنَّنا
نسينا تحيَّةَ نعناعنا حولنا ، ونسينا
السلامَ السريعَ على غدِنا بعدنا . . .
كان حبرُ الظهيرة أبيضَ ، لولا
كتابُ الفراشةِ من حولنا . . .

يا فراشةُ! يا أُختَ نفسك ، كوني
كما شئت ، قبلَ حنيني وبعد حنيني .
ولكنْ خُذيني أخاً لجناحك يَبْقَ جنوني
معي ساخنًا! يا فراشةُ! يا أُمَّ
نفسك ، لا تتركيني لِما صَمَّمَ الحرفيُّون
لي من صناديقَ . . . لا تتركيني!

من سماءٍ إلى أُختها يعبرُ الحالمونْ
حاملين مرايا من الماء حاشيةً للفراشة
في وسعنا أن نكون كما ينبغي أن نكون
من سماءٍ
إلى أُختها
يعبرُ الحالمونْ

The butterfly weaves with a needle of light
the decoration of its comedy
The butterfly is born of itself
And dances in the flames of its tragedy

Half-phoenix. What touches it touches us. A dark
figure between fire and light . . . Between two paths.
No. Our love is neither frivolity nor wisdom. It is
like that, always like that . . . like that
From one sky
    to another
        dreamers pass . . .

The butterfly, water that longs to fly. It flutters away
from the sweat of young girls. It grows in a cloud
of memories. The butterfly is what the poem doesn't say
So delicately it breaks words, like
the dream breaks the dreamers . . .

It shall be . . .
Our tomorrow shall be present with us
and our past present with us
Our day present

ألفراشةُ تنسجُ من إبرة الضوء
زينة ملهاتها
ألفراشةُ تُولَدُ من ذاتها
والفراشةُ ترقصُ في نار مأساتِها

نصفُ عنقاءَ . ما مَسَّها مَسُّنا : شَبَهٌ
داكنٌ بين ضوءٍ ونار . . . وبين طريقين .
لا . ليس طيشًا ولاَّ حكمةً حُبُّنا
هكذا دائمًا ، هكذا . . . هكذا
من سماءٍ
إلى أُختها
يعبرُ الحالمون . . .

ألفراشةُ ماءٌ يحنُّ إلى الطيران . ويُفْلِتُ
من عَرَق الفتيات ، وينبتُ في غيمةِ
الذكريات . الفراشةُ ما لا تقولُ القصيدةُ ،
من فَرْطِ خفَّتها تَكْسِرُ الكلماتِ ، كما
يكسرُ الحُلُمُ الحالمين . . .

وليكن . .
وليكن غدُنا حاضرًا معنا
وليكن حاضرًا أمسُنا معنا
وليكن يَوْمُنا حاضرًا

at this afternoon's banquet prepared
for the feast of the butterfly, so that the dreamers may pass
from one sky to another . . . safe and sound

From one sky to another dreamers pass . . .

في وليمةِ هذا النّهار المُعَدِّ

لعيدِ الفراشة ، كي يَعبر الحالمون

من سماءٍ إلى أُختها . . . سالمين

من سماءٍ إلى أُختها يعُبُرُ الحالمون . . .

One Traveler Said to Another:
We Won't Return As . . .

I don't know the desert
But I planted words at its edges . . .
The words said what they said, and I left
like a divorced woman, like her broken husband
I kept nothing but the rhythm
I hear it
and follow it
and lift it, doves
on the path to the sky
the sky of my song
I am a son of the Syrian plain
I live there, traveling or residing
among the people of the sea
But the mirage presses me eastward
to the ancient Bedouin
I lead the beautiful horses to water
I feel the pulse of the alphabet in the echo
I return a window looking out in two directions . . .
I forget who I am so that I can be
plural in the singular and in time
with the praises of the foreign sailors under my windows,
so that I can be the warring parties' letter to their families:
We won't return as we went

قال المُسافر للمسافر :
لن نعود كما . . .

لا أَعرفُ الصحراءَ ،
لكنِّي نَبَتُّ على جوانبها كلاما . . .
قال الكلامُ كلامَهُ ، ومضيتُ
كامرأة مُطَلَّقة مضيت كزوجها المكسورِ ،
لم أحفظْ سوَى الإيقاع
أَسمعُهُ
وأتبعُهُ
وأرفعُهُ يماما
في الطَّريق إلى السماء ،
سماء أُغنيتي ،
أنا ابنُ الساحل السوريِّ ،
أُسكنُهُ رحيلاً أو مُقاما
بينَ أهل البحر ،
لكنَّ السرابَ يشدُّني شرقًا
إلى البَدْو القُدامى ،
أُورِدُ الخيلَ الجميلةَ ماءَها ،
وأجسُّ نَبْضَ الأَبديَّة في الصَّدى ،
وأعودُ نافذةً على جهتَيْن . . .
أنسى مَن أكونُ لكي أَكونَ
جماعةٌ في واحد ، ومُعَاصرًا
لمدائح البحَّارة الغُرباء تحت نوافذي ،
ورسالةَ المتحاربينَ إلى ذويهمْ :
لن نَعُودَ كما ذهَبْنا

We won't return . . . even secretly!
I don't know the desert
however often it's haunted me
In the desert absence said to me:
Write!
I said: There is another writing on the mirage
It said: Write and the mirage will become green
I said: I lack absence
I said: I still haven't learned the words
It said to me: Write and you'll know them
and know where you were, and where you are
and how you came, and who you will be tomorrow
Put your name in my hand and write
so you'll know who I am and will go, a cloud
into the open . . .
So I wrote: Whoever writes his story will inherit
the land of words, and possess meaning, entirely!
I don't know the desert
but I bid it farewell: Peace
to the tribe east of my song: Peace
to the descendants, in their plurality, upon the sword: Peace
to my mother's son under his palm tree: Peace
to the ode that preserved our planets: Peace
to the passing peoples, a memory for my memory: Peace
to "peace be upon me," between two poems:
one that has been written
and another whose poet died of passion!

لن نَعُودَ . . . . ولو لماما!

لا أعرفُ الصحراءَ ،

مهما زُرْتُ هاجسَها ،

وفي الصحراء قالَ الغَيْبُ لي :

أكتُبْ!

فقُلْتُ : على السَّراب كتابةٌ أُخرى

فقال : أكتُبْ ليخضرَّ السرابُ

فقُلْتُ : ينقُصُني الغيابُ

وقُلْتُ : لم أتعلَّم الكلمات بَعْدُ

فقال لي : أُكْتُبْ لتعرفها

وتعرف أين كنتَ ، وأيْنَ أنتَ

وكيف جئتَ ، ومَنْ تكونُ غَدًا ،

ضع اسْمَكَ في يَدِيْ واكْتُبْ

لتعرف مَنْ أنا ، واذهبْ غماما

في المدى . . . .

فكتبتُ : مَنْ يكتُبْ حكايته يَرِثْ

أرضَ الكلام ، ويْمْلُك المعنى تماما!

لا أعرفُ الصحراءَ ،

لكنّي أودِّعُها : سلاما

للقبيلة شَرْقَ أُغنيتي : سلاما

للسُلالة في تعدُّدها على سَيْف : سلاما

لابن أُمّي تحت نَخْلَتِه : سلاما

للمُعَلَّقة التي حفظتْ كواكبَنا : سلاما

للشعوب ثمرُ ذاكرةٌ لذاكرتي : سلاما

للسلام عليَّ بين قصيدتين :

قصيدة كُتِبَتْ

وأُخرى ماتَ شاعرُها غراما!

Am I me?
Am I there . . . or here?
In each you, me
I am you, the second person. It is not exile
for me to be you. It is not exile
for my me to be you. And it is not exile
for the sea and the desert to be
the song of the traveler to the traveler:
I won't return, as I went,
I won't return . . . even secretly!

أَأَنا أَنا؟

أَأَنا هُنالك . . . أَم هُنا؟

في كُلِّ «أَنتَ» أَنا ،

أَنا أَنتَ المُخاطَبُ ، ليس منفَى

أَن أَكونَك . ليس منفَى

أَن تكونَ أَنايَ أَنتَ . وليسَ منفَى

أَن يكون البحرُ والصحراءُ

أُغنيةَ المسافر للمسافر :

لَنْ أَعودَ ، كما ذَهَبْتُ ،

ولن أَعُودَ . . . ولَو لماما!

A Rhyme for the Odes

No one led me to myself. I am the guide, the guide
to myself between the sea and the desert. I was born of my language
on the route of India tucked between two small tribes. Above them was
the ancient religions' moon and the impossible peace
They had to grasp the astrology of their neighbor Persia
and the great anxiety of the Romans so that the burdened time
would release itself over the Arab tent. Who am I? This
is the others' question. It doesn't have an answer. I am my language
I am an ode . . . two odes . . . ten. This is my language
I am my language. I am what the words said:
Be
my body. So I was a body for their voice. I am what
I said to the words: Be the crossroads between my body
and the eternal desert. Be so that I will be as I say!
There is no land to carry me above the earth so my speech carries me,
a bird spreads out from me, building its journey nest before me
in my debris, in the debris of the magical world that surrounds me,
upon a wind, I rose. My long night took its time
. . . This is my language, collars of stars around the necks
of lovers: they left
they took place and left
they took time and left
they took their scent from the clay pots
and the short grass and left

قافية من أجل المعلَّقات

ما دَلَّني أَحَدٌ عَلَيَّ . أنا الدليلُ ، أنا الدليلُ
إليَّ بين البحر والصحراء . من لُغتي وُلدتُ
على طريق الهند بين قبيلتَين صغيرتَين عليهما
قَمَرُ الديانات القديمة ، والسلامُ المستحيلْ
وعليهما أن تحفظا فَلَكَ الجوار الفارسيِّ
وهاجسَ الرّوم الكبيرَ ، ليهبطَ الزّمن الثقيلْ
عن خيمة العربيِّ أَكْثَرَ . من أنا؟ هذا
سؤالُ الآخرين ولا جوابَ له . أنا لُغَتي أنا ،
وأنا مُعَلَّقَةٌ . . . مُعَلَّقتان . . . عَشْرٌ ، هذه لغَتي
أنا لغَتي . أنا ما قالت الكلماتُ :
كُنْ
جَسَدي ، فكُنْتُ لِنَبْرِها جَسَدًا . أنا ما
قُلْتُ للكلمات : كُوني ملتقى جَسَدي مع
الأَبديَّة الصحراء . كُوني كَي أكونَ كما أقولُ!
لا أَرضَ فوقَ الأرض تحملني ، فيحملني كلامي
طائرًا متفرِّعًا مني ، وبيني عش رحلته أمامي
في حُطامي ، في حطام العالم السحريِّ من حَولي ،
على ريح وَقَفْتُ . وطالَ بي ليلي الطويلْ
. . . هذه لغَتي قلائد من نُجوم حول أعناق
الأَحبَّة : هاجروا
أخذوا المكان وهاجروا
أخذوا الزَّمان وهاجروا
أخذوا روائحَهُمْ عَن الفخّار
والكَلأَ الشّحيح ، وهاجروا

They took the words, and the bruised heart left
with them. Does the echo, this echo,
this white sound mirage, allow for a name whose hoarseness
fills the unknown, that departure fills, divinely?
The sky places me in a window, so I look
I see no one but myself . . .
I find myself inside-out,
a double of myself. And my visions
are not far from the desert
My steps are of wind and sand
My world is my body and what my hands possess
I am the traveler and the path
Gods reveal themselves to me, and then go. We don't draw out
our conversation about what is to come. There is no tomorrow
in this desert but what we saw yesterday
So I'll lift my ode so that cyclical time will break
and beautiful days will be born!
All that has passed will come tomorrow
I leave myself to itself, having taken its fill of the present
The departure empties me
of temples. The sky has its peoples and its wars
As for me, I have a gazelle as a wife, and palms as
odes in the book of sand. A past is what I see
Man possesses the kingdom of dust and its crown. My language
will triumph over time – the enemy, over my progeny,
over me, over my father, and over an end that doesn't end
This is my language and my miracle. My magic disobeys.

أخذوا الكلامَ وهاجَرَ القلبُ القتيلُ
مَعَهُم . أيتَّسِعُ الصَّدى ، هذا الصدى ،
هذا السرابُ الأبيضُ الصوتيُّ لاسم تملأ
المجهولَ بُحَّتُهُ ، ويملأُهُ الرحيلُ أُلوهةٌ؟
تضعُ السماءُ عليَّ نافذةً فأنظرُ : لا
أرى أحدًا سوايَ . . .
وجدتُ نفسي عندَ خارجها
كما كانت معي ، ورؤايَ
لا تنأى عن الصحراء ،
من ريح ومن رمل خُطايَ
وعالمي جَسَدي وما مَلَكَتْ يدايَ
أنا المُسافر والسبيلُ
يُطِلُّ آلهةً عليَّ ويذهبون ، ولا نُطيل
حديثَنا عمّا سيأتي . لا غَدُ في
هذه الصحراء إلّا ما رأينا أمس ،
فلأرفعْ مُعَلَّقتي لينكسرَ الزّمانُ الدائريُّ
ويُولَدَ الوقتُ الجميلُ!
ما أَكْثَرَ الماضي يجيء غدًا
تركتُ لنفسِها نفسي الّتي امتلأتْ بحاضرها
وأفرغني الرحيلُ
من المعابد . للسماء شعوبُها وحروبُها
أمَّا أنا ، فليَ الغزالةُ زوجةً ، وليَ النخيلُ
معلّقات في كتاب الرّمل . ماضٍ ما أرى
للمرء مملكةُ الغُبار وتاجُهُ . فلتنتصِرْ
لُغتي على الدَّهر العَدوّ ، على سُلَالاتي ،
عليَّ ، على أبي ، وعلى زَوَالٍ لا يزولُ
هذِهِ لُغتي ومُعْجزَتي . عصًا سِحْري .

Gardens are my Babylon and my obelisk, my first identity,
my polished metal
The sacred of the Arab in the desert
worships what flows
from rhymes, like the stars on its cloak
and worships what it tells

Prose, then, is inevitable
A divine prose, so the Prophet will triumph . . .

حدائقُ بابلي ومسلَّتي ، وهويّتي الأُولى ،
ومعدَني الصقيلُ
ومقدَّسُ العربيِّ في الصحراءِ ،
يعبُدُ ما يسيلُ
من القوافي كالنجوم على عَبَاءَتِه ،
ويعبُدُ ما يقولُ

لا بُدَّ من نثرٍ إذًا ،
لا بُدَّ من نثرٍ إلهيٍّ لينتصرَ الرَّسُولُ . . .

The Sparrow, as it is . . .

Tradition's perplexity: This spilled out dusk
calls me to its lightness behind the pane
I rarely dreamt of you, oh sparrow
A wing didn't dream of a wing . . .
Each of us, disquiet

You have what I don't: Blueness is your woman
And the return of the wind to the wind, your shelter
Soar! The way the spirit within thirsts
for the spirit. Clap for the days that your feathers
weave. Abandon me, if you like
for my house, like my words, is narrow

It knows the roof like a welcome guest. It knows
the basil pot that sits like a grandmother at
her window . . . It knows where the water and bread are
And the trap set for the mice . . .
Its wings tremble like a woman's shawl as she slips away
It flies, blue . . .

الدوري ، كما هو كما هو . . .

حَيْرَةُ التَّقليد : هذا الغَسَقُ المُهَرَقُ
يَدْعُوني إلى خِفّته خلفَ زُجاج
الضَّوء . لم أُحْلَمْ كثيرًا بكَ ، يا
دوريُّ . لم يُحْلْ جناحٌ بجناحٍ . . .
وكلانا قَلَقُ

لَكَ ما ليس ليَ : الزُّرْقَةُ أُنثاكَ
ومأواكَ رجوعُ الرّيحِ للرّيح ،
فحلّقْ! مثلما تعطشُ في الروحُ
للرّوح ، وصَفِّقْ للنّهارات التي ينسجها
ريشُكَ ، واهجرني إذا شئتَ
فَبَيْتي ، ككلامي ، ضَيِّقُ

يألَفُ السَّقْفَ ، كضيف مَرح ، يألَفُ
حَوْضَ الحَبَقِ الجالسَ ، كالجُدّة ، في
نافذة . . . يعرفُ أينَ الماءُ والخبزُ ،
وأينَ الشَّرَكُ المنصوبُ للفأر . . .
ويهتزُّ جناحاهُ كشال امرأةٍ تفلت منّا ،
ويطيرُ الأَزرَقُ . . .

This celebration, hasty, like me
scrapes out a heart and tosses it onto the straw
Is there a tremor that lingers a single day
in the silver cup?
There's no humor in my mail
You'll come, sparrow, however much
the earth narrows and the horizon overflows

What do your wings take from me?
Tighten and disappear like a fleeing afternoon
A grain of wheat would free
its wings. What do my mirrors take
from you? Sky would allow
the absolute to see my spirit

You are free. I am free. Each of us loves
what is absent. Descend, so I'll rise. Rise
so I'll descend. Oh sparrow! Give me light's
bell. I'll give you a home fit for time
We'll complete each other
between a sky and a sky
when we part!

نَزِقٌ مِثْلِي هذا الاحتفالُ النَّدِقُ
يخمش القلب ويَرْميه على القَشّ ،
أما من رَعْشَة تمكّثُ في آنية
الفضَّة يومًا واحدًا؟!
وبريدي فارغٌ من أيِّ مَلْهَاةٍ ،
ستأتي ، أيُّها الدوريُّ ، مهما
ضاقتِ الأرضُ وفاضَ الأُفُقُ

ما الذي يأخذُهُ منِّي جناحاكَ؟
توتَّرٌ ، وتبخُّرٌ كنهار طائِشٍ
لا بُدَّ من حبَّةِ قمحٍ ليكون
الريشُ حُرًّا . ما الذي تأخذُهُ منك
مراياي؟ ولا بُدَّ لروحي مِنْ
سماءٍ ، ليراها المُطلَقُ

أنتَ حُرٌّ . وأنا حُرٌّ . كلانا يَعْشَقُ
الغائبَ . فلتهبطْ لكي أصعَدَ . ولتصْعَدْ
لكي أهبط . يا دوريُّ! هَبْني جَرَسَ
الضَّوء ، أهَبْك المنزل المأهولَ بالوقتِ .
كلانا يُكْمِلُ الآخَرَ ،
ما بين سماءٍ وسماءٍ ،
عندما نفترقُ!

V.

Rain on the Church Tower

مطرٌ فوق برج الكنيسة

Helen: What a Rain

I met Helen on Tuesday
at three o'clock
the hour of infinite tedium
But the rain's voice
with a woman like Helen
is a hymn for travel

Rain
what a longing . . . the longing of the sky
for itself!
Rain
What a wail . . . the wail of the wolf
for its kind!

Rain upon the roof of dryness,
dryness gilded on the church's icons
– How far is the land from me?
How far is love from you?
The stranger says to Helen, the bread seller,
on a street, narrow like her stockings
– It's no further than a word . . . and a rain!

هيلين ، يا لَهُ من مطر

إلتَقَيْتُ بهيلينَ ، يَوْمَ الثّلاثاء
في السّاعة الثالثةْ
ساعة الضّجَر اللّانهائيِّ ،
لكنَّ صَوْت المَطَرْ ،
مَعَ أُنثى كهيلينَ
ترنيمةٌ للسَفَرْ

مَطَرٌ ،
يا لَهُ من حنينٍ . . . حنينِ السّماء
إلى نفسِها!
مَطَرٌ ،
يا لَهُ من أنينٍ . . . أنينِ الذّئابِ
على جِنْسِها!

مَطَرٌ فوقَ سقف الجفاف ،
الجفاف المُذَهَّب في أيْقُونات الكنائس ،
– كَم تَبْعُدُ الأرضُ عنّي؟
وكَمْ يبعُدُ الحُبُّ عنك؟
يقول الغريبُ لبائعة الخُبز ، هيلينَ ،
في شارع ضَيِّقٍ مثل جَوْرَبِها ،
– ليسَ أكثرَ مِن لَفْظَةٍ . . . ومَطَرْ!

Rain hungry for trees . . .
Rain hungry for stone . . .

The stranger says to the bread seller:
Helen, Helen! Is the aroma of the bread
rising from you, now, to a balcony
in a distant country . . .
to replace Homer's words?
Is water rising from your shoulders to
parched trees in a poem?

She says to him: What a rain
What a rain!

The stranger says to Helen: I need
Narcissus to gaze at the water,
your water, in my body. If you stare, Helen,
into the water of our dreams . . . you'll find
the dead, on your two shores, singing your name:
Helen . . . Helen! Don't leave us
alone like the moon

What a rain
What a rain!

مَطَرٌ جائعٌ للشَّجَرْ . . .

مَطَرٌ جائعٌ للحَجَرْ . . .

ويقولُ الغريبُ لبائعة الخُبز :

هيلينُ هيلينُ! هل تصعَدُ الآنَ

رائحةُ الخُبز منكِ ، إلى شرفةٍ

في بلادٍ بعيدةْ . . .

لتنسخَ أقوالَ «هُوميرَ»؟

هل يصعَدُ الماءُ من كتفَيْكِ إلى

شَجَرٍ يابسٍ في قصيدةْ؟

تقول لَهُ : يا لَهُ مِنْ مَطَرْ

يا لَهُ مِنْ مَطَرْ!

ويقولُ الغريبُ لهيلينَ : يَنْقُصُني

نَرْجِسٌ كي أُحَدِّقَ في الماء ،

مائلِكِ ، في جَسَدي . حَدِّقي أنتِ

هيلينُ في ماء أحلامنا . . . تَجدي

الميتين على ضَفَّتَيْكِ يُغَنُّون لاسْمكِ :

هيلينُ . . . هيلينُ! لا تتْرُكينا

وَحيدين مِثْلَ القَمَرْ

– يا لَهُ من مَطَرْ

يا لَهُ من مطرْ !

The stranger says to Helen: I used to fight
in your two trenches, and you haven't recovered from my Asiatic
blood. You haven't recovered from the black
blood flowing in the veins of your roses. Helen!
How stern the Greeks were then
How tough Ulysses was, a solitary driven to travel
in search of his myth!

What I didn't say to Helen I said
to others, and what I said to others
I didn't say to Helen. But Helen
knows what the stranger doesn't say . . .
She knows what the stranger says to a scent
broken up in the rain
She says to him:
The Trojan War didn't happen
It never did
Never . . .
What a rain
What a rain!

ويقولُ الغريبُ لهيلينَ : كُنْتُ أُحاربُ
في خَنْدَقَيْكِ ، ولم تَبْرَئي من دمي
الآسْيَوِيِّ . ولَن تبرَئي من دم
مُبْهَم في شرايين وَرْدِكِ . هيلينْ!
كَمْ كَانَ إغريقُ ذاكَ الزمان قُسَاةً ،
وكَم كانَ «أوليسُ» وَحْشًا يُحبُّ السَفَرْ
باحثًا عن خُرَافته في السَفَرْ!

الكلامُ الذي لم أَقُلْهُ لها
قُلْتُهُ . والكلامُ الذي قُلْتُهُ
لم أَقُلْهُ لهيلينَ . لكنَّ هيلينَ
تعرفُ ما لا يقولُ الغريبُ . . .
وتعرفُ ماذا يقول الغريب لرائحةٍ
تتكسَّرُ تحت المَطَرْ ،
فتقول لَهُ :
حَرْبُ طروادة لم تَكُنْ
لم تكن أبدًا
أبدًا . . .
يا لَهُ مِنْ مَطَرْ
يا لَهُ من مَطَرْ!

Night Overflowing the Body

Jasmine on a July night. A song
for two strangers who meet on a road
leading nowhere . . .
Who am I, after two almond eyes, he says
Who am I, after your exile in me, she says
So, fine, lets be careful not to
stir the salt of the ancient seas in a body that remembers . . .
She would return to him her warm body
He would return to her his warm body
Like this the lovers, strangers, would leave their love
disheveled, the way they leave their underwear
between the sheet's petals . . .
– If you're really my lover, compose
a song of songs for me, and etch my name
into the trunk of a pomegranate tree in the gardens of Babylon
– If you really love me, put
my dream in my hands and say to him, to Mary's son:
How could you do to us what you did to yourself?
Sir, do we have enough justice so that we'll
be just tomorrow?
– How might I be healed of jasmine, tomorrow?
– How might I be healed of jasmine, tomorrow?
They surrender to darkness, together, in shadows that dance across
the ceiling of his room: Don't be somber
toward my breasts, she said to him . . .

ليلٌ يفيضُ من الجَسَد

ياسمينٌ على لَيْلِ تَموزَ ، أُغْنِيَّةٌ
لِغَريبَيْنِ يلتقيان على شارعٍ
لا يُؤدِّي إلى هَدَف . . .
مَنْ أنا بعد عينينِ لوزِيَّتينِ؟ يقول الغريب
مَنْ أنا بعد منفاكَ فِيَّ؟ تقولُ الغريبة .
إذنْ ، حسنًا ، فلنكُنْ حذرَينِ لئلا
نُحرِّكَ ملْحَ البحار القديمة في جَسَدٍ يتذكَّر . . .
كانت تُعيدُ لَهُ جَسَدًا ساخنًا ،
ويُعيدُ لها جَسَدًا ساخنًا .
هكذا يتركُ العاشقان الغريبان حُبَّهما
فَوْضَوِيًّا ، كما يتركان ثيابَهما الدّاخليَّةَ
بينَ زُهور الملاءات . . .
- إن كُنْتَ حقًا حبيبي ، فألِّفْ
نشيدَ أناشيدَ لِيْ ، واحفُرْ اسمي
على جِذْعِ رُمّانَةٍ في حدائق بابلَ . . .
- إن كُنْتَ حقًّا تُحِبِّينَني ، فضَعي
حُلُمي في يدَيَّ . وقولي لَهُ ، لابن مريمَ ،
كيفَ فَعَلْتَ بنا ما فعلتَ بنفسك ،
يا سيِّدي ، هل لدينا من العَدْلِ ما سوف يكفي
ليجعلَنا عادلين غدًا؟
- كيف أُشفى من الياسمين غدًا؟
- كيف أُشفى من الياسمين غدًا؟
يُعتمان معًا في ظلالٍ تشعُّ على
سقفِ غُرْفَتِه : لا تكُنْ مُعْتِمًا
بَعْدَ نهدَيَّ - قالت له . . .

He said: Your breasts are the night that lights up the drudgery
Night that covers me in kisses, and fills us both up,
the place and I, with night overflowing the cup . . .
She laughs at his words. She laughs again
as she hides the slope of the night in her hand . . .
– Oh my lover, if I could
have been a boy, I would have been you
– If I could have been a girl
I would have been you!
She cries, as she usually does, returning
from a wine-colored sky: Take me,
stranger, to a country upon whose willow
I won't have a bluebird!
She cries, to cut across her forests in her long
departure toward herself: Who am I?
Who am I after your long exile in my body?
Ah this exile from me, from you, from my country
– Who am I after these two almond eyes?
Show me my tomorrow!
Like this the lovers leave their farewells
disheveled, like the scent of jasmine on a July night . . .
Every July jasmine carries me to
a street leading nowhere
Yet I continue my song:
Jasmine
on a
July
night . . .

قال : نهداك ليلٌ يُضيءُ الضروريَّ

نهداك ليلٌ يُقَبِّلُني ، وامتلأنا أنا

والمكانُ بليلٍ يَفيضُ منَ الكَأسِ . . .

تَضْحكُ من وَصْفِه . ثمَّ تضحك أكثَرَ

حين تُخَبِّئُ مُنْحَدَرَ اللّيل في يَدها . . .

- يا حبيبيَ ، لَو كان لي

أَنْ أكونَ صَبيًّا . . . لكُنْتُكَ أنتَ

- ولو كان لي أنْ أكونَ فتاةً

لكنتُك أنتِ! . . .

وتبكي ، كعادَتها ، عندَ عَوْدَتِها

من سماءٍ نبيذيَّةِ اللّونِ : خُذْني

إلى بَلَدٍ ليسَ لي طائرٌ أزرقُ

فوقَ صَفْصافِه يا غَريبُ!

وتبكي ، لتَقْطَعَ غاباتِها في الرّحيلِ

الطويلِ إلى ذاتِها : مَنْ أنا؟

مَنْ أنا بعد مَنْفاكَ في جَسدي؟

آهِ مِنِّي ، ومنكَ ، ومن بلدي

- مَنْ أنا بعد عينين لوزيَّتين؟

أَريني غَدي! . . .

هكذا يتركُ العاشقان وداعَهُما

فَوْضويًّا ، كرائحةِ الياسمين على ليلِ تَمُّوزَ . . .

في كُلِّ تمُّوزَ يَحملُني الياسمينُ إلى

شارعٍ ، لا يؤدِّي إلى هَدَفٍ ،

بَيْدَ أَنِّي أُتابعُ أغنيَّتي :

ياسمينٌ

على

ليلِ

تمُّوزَ . . . . .

To the Gypsy, a Well-tuned Sky

You leave the wind, ailing, on Mulberry trees
As for me
I'll walk to the sea the way I breathe
Why have you done what you've done to us? Why
did you tire of staying, oh gypsy
in the iris' quarter?

We have what you want of gold and cavalier
blood in our lineage. Knock with your heel
on the icon of being and birds will descend to you. There are
angels . . . and a well-tuned sky. So do what
you please! If you knock on hearts like a nutcracker,
the horses' blood will shimmer!

There's no country for your hair. No home for the wind. No
roof for me in the Pleiades of your breasts. From a laughing
lilac circling your night. Alone I traverse your constellation
As if you'd sculpted
yourself, oh gypsy
What have you done with our clay since that year?

للغجريّة ، سماء مُدَرَّبة

تَتْرُكِينَ الهواءَ مريضًا على شَجَرِ التوتِ ،
أمّا أنا
فسأمشي إلى البحر كيف أتنفَّسْ
لماذا فعَلْت بنا ما فعَلْت . . . لماذا
مَلَلْت الإقامة ، يا غجريَّةُ ،
في حارةِ السَوْسَنةْ؟

عِنْدَنا ما تُريدينَ مِنْ ذَهَب ودَم
طائش في السُلالات . دُقّي بكَعْب حذائِك
أيقونةَ الكون تهبطْ إليك الطيورُ . هناك
ملائكةٌ . . . وسماءٌ مُدَرَّبة ، فاصنَعِني ما
تشائين! دُقِّي القُلوبَ ككِسَارة الجوز
يَبْزُغْ دَمُ الأَحصنةْ!

لا بلادَ لشِعرك . لا بَيْتَ للريح . لا
سَقْفَ لي في ثُرَيَّات صَدْرِك . من لَيْلَكِ
ضاحك حول لَيْلِكِ أَسْلُكُ دَرْبَ
الشُّعَيْرات وحدي . كأنَّكِ مِنْ صُنْع
نَفسِك ، يا غجريَّةُ ،
ماذا صَنَعْتِ بصلصالِنا منذ تلك السَنةْ؟

You put on the place as if you were putting on flaming garments,
hastily. The earth beneath your hands
can only turn toward departure's instruments: Anklets
for water. A guitar for air. A flute so India will grow
more distant. Oh gypsy, don't leave us like
an army leaves its sad traces!

When, from lands of swallows, you descended to us
we opened our doors to eternity, obedient. Your tents
are guitars for vagabonds. We rise and dance until the
setting sun bleeds upon your feet. Your tents
are a guitar for the horses of the ancient conquerors who attack
to create the places' myth

With each strum her *djinn* touched us. We moved
to another time. We broke our pitchers one
by one, to accompany her rhythm. We were neither good
nor evil, like in the stories. She would
dictate our fates with her ten fingers
thrumming . . . thrumming!

A cloud, carried from our sleep by doves
Will it return tomorrow? No. They say:
The gypsy never returns. She doesn't cross the same country

تَرْتَدِينَ المكانَ كما ترتدينَ سراويلَ نار
على عَجَل . لا وظيفةَ للأرض تحتَ يديكِ
سوى الالتفاتِ إلى أدواتِ الرّحيل : خلاخيلَ
للماء . جيتارة للهواء ، وناي لتبتعدَ
الهندُ أكثرَ . يا غجريّةُ لا تَتْرُكينا كما
يترُكُ الجيشُ آثارَهُ الحْزنةْ!

عندما ، في نواحي السّنونو ، هبطتِ علينا
فَتَحْنا على الأبديّةِ أبوابَنا صاغرين . خيامُكِ
جيتارةٌ للصّعاليك . نَعلو ونرقُص حتى مغيبِ
الغروبِ المُدَمَّى على قَدَمَيْكِ . خيامُكِ
جيتارةٌ لخيولِ الغُزاةِ القدامى تَكِرُّ
لتصنع أسطورَةَ الأمكنةْ

كُلّما حَرّكَتْ وَتَرًا مَسَّنا جنُّها . وانتقلنا
إلى زَمَنٍ آخر . وكَسَرْنا أباريقنا ، واحدًا
واحدًا ، لنُصاحبَ إيقاعَها . لم نَكُنْ طيّبينَ
ولا سيّئينَ ، كما في الرّوايات . كانت
تُسَيِّرُ أقدارَنا بأصابعها العَشْرِ ،
دندنةً . . . دندنةْ!

غيمةً ، حَمَلَتْها اليماماتُ من نومنا
هل تعودُ غدًا؟ لا . يقولون : لا
ترجعُ الغجريّةُ . لا تَعْبُرُ الغجريّةُ في بَلَدٍ

twice. Who, then, will wed the horses of this
place to their kind? Who, after
her, will polish the places' silver?

مَرَّتين . فمَن سيزفُّ ، إذًا ، خَيْلَ هذا
المكان إلى جِنْسِها؟ من يُلمِّعُ مِنْ
بعدِها فِضَّةَ الأَمكنةْ؟

First Lessons on a Spanish guitar

Two guitars
exchange a *muwashah*
and tear
with the silk of their desperation
the marble of our absence
from our door
and make the evergreens dance

Two guitars . . .

A blue eternity carries us
Two clouds sink
into the sea, near you
Then two waves rise
over the steps, licking your strides,
and set aflame
the salt of the shores in my blood
and migrate
to purple's clouds!

Two guitars . . .

تمارينٌ أُولى على جيتارة إسبانيّة

جيتارتانْ
تَتَبادَلانِ مُوَشَّحًا
وتُقَطِّعانْ
بحريرٍ يأْسهما
رُخامَ غيابنا
عن بابنا ،
وتُرَقِّصانِ السنديانْ

جيتارتانْ . . .

أَبديّةٌ زَرْقاءُ تحملُنا ،
وتسقُطُ غيمتانْ
في البحر قُرْبَكَ ،
ثمَّ تصعدُ مَوْجَتانْ
فَوْقَ السَلالمِ ، تَلْحَسانِ خُطاكَ
فوقَ ، وتُضْرمانْ
مِلْحَ الشَّواطئ في دمي
وتُهَاجرانِ
إلى غيوم الأُرجوانْ!

جيتارتانْ . . .

Water and stone and saffron cry
The wind cries:
"Our tomorrow is no longer ours . . ."
A shadow cries behind the hysteria of a horse
touched by a string, closed in on by the distance
between the blades and the abyss
So it chooses the arc of ardor

Two guitars . . .

A white song for the dark girl:
Time breaks up
so that its palanquin will pass two armies:
Egyptian and Hittite
The smoke rises
the smoke of its colored ornaments
over the rubble of the place . . .

Two guitars . . .

Only the notes of the *Nahawand* will take from you
the Andalus of time and the
Samarkand of yesteryear:

الماءُ يَبْكي ، والحَصَى ، والزعفرانْ

والرّيحُ تبكي :

«لم يَعُد غَدُنا لنا . . .»

والظلُّ يبكي خَلْفَ هِسْتِيرْيا حصانٍ

مَسَّهُ وَتَرٌ ، وضاقَ به المَدَى

بين المَدَى والهاويةٌ ،

فاخْتارَ قَوْسَ العُنْفُوانْ

جيتارتانْ . . .

أُغنيَّةٌ بيضاءُ للسمراءِ ،

ينكسرُ الزمانْ

لِيمُرَّ هَوْدَجُها على جَيْشَينِ :

مِصْريٌّ ، وحِثّيٌّ

ويرتفعُ الدّخانْ

دخانٌ زينتها المُلَوَّنُ

فوقَ أنقاضِ المكانْ . . .

جيتارتانْ . . .

لا شيءَ يأْخُذُ مِنْك أَندَلُسَ الزّمانِ

ولا سَمَرْقَنْدَ الزّمانْ

إلّا خُطى النَهَوَنْد :

a gazelle leaving its funeral procession behind
flying on the wind of the daisy
Oh love! Oh my ill illness
Enough, enough!
Don't leave your grave
on my mare again
Two guitars will slaughter us here

Two guitars . . .
Two guitars . . .

تلكَ غزالةٌ سَبَقَتْ جنازَتَها
وطارتْ في مَهَبّ الأُقحوانْ
يا حُبُّ! يا مَرَضي المريضَ
كفَى ، كَفى!
لا تَنْسَ قَبْرَكَ مَرَّةً أُخرى
على فَرَسي ،
ستذبحُنا هنا جيتارتانْ

جيتارتان . . .
جيتارتان . . .

The Seven Days of Love

Tuesday: Phoenix

Your passing by the words would be enough
for the phoenix to find its image in us, and for the spirit,
born of the spirit, to give birth to a body . . .
A body is needed for the spirit to consume it,
with itself, for itself. A body is needed
for the spirit to show what it's hidden from eternity
Let's burn up, for nothing, but to unite!

Wednesday: Narcissus

Her age, twenty-five women. Born
as she wished to be, walking around her image
in the water, as if it were another's. I need
a night, to run within myself. I need
a love to jump over the tower. She drew away
from her shadow, so lightening would pass between the two
like a stranger passes through his poem . . .

أَيَّامُ الحُبِّ السبعة

الثلاثاء : عنقاء

يكفي مُرورُك بالأَلفاظ كي تَجِدَ
العنقاءُ صُورَتها فينا ، وكي تَلِدَ
الروحُ التي وُلِدتْ من روحها جسدا . . .
لا بُدَّ من جَسَد للروح يَحرِقُهُ
بنفسها ولها ، لا بُدَّ من جَسَد
لتُظْهِرَ الروحُ ما أَخفَتْ مِنَ الأَبد
فلنحترِقْ ، لا لشيءٍ ، بل لنتَّحِدا!

الأربعاء : نرجِسَة

خمسٌ وعشرونَ أُنثى عُمْرُها . وُلِدتْ
كما تريدُ . . . وتَمشي حولَ صُورَتها
كأنها غيرُها في الماء : ينقُصُني
ليلٌ . . . لأركضَ في نَفْسي . وينقصني
حُبٌّ لأَقفزَ فوقَ البرج . . . وابتعَدَتْ
عن ظلِّها ، ليمُرَّ بينهما
كما يمُرُّ غريبٌ في قصيدتِه . . .

Thursday: Genesis

I found myself, inside and out of myself,
with you, between the two, a mirror . . .
The earth visits you, sometimes, seeking its finery
It visits you to climb to the root of the dream
As for me, I can be as
you left me yesterday, near the water, split
into earth and sky. Ah . . . but where are they?

Friday: Another Winter

If you go far, hang my dream
on the chest of drawers, a souvenir of you or of
me. Another winter will come. And I'll see
two doves on the chair, and I'll see
what you did with the coconut: Milk flowed
from my words onto another carpet

If you go, then, take winter!

الخميس : تكوين

وجدتُ نَفْسِيَ في نَفسي وخارجها
وأنت بَيْنَهُما المرأةُ بينهما . . .
تَزُورُكَ الأَرضُ أحيانًا لزينتها
وللصُّعود إلى ما سَبَّبَ الحُلُما .
أمَّا أَنا ، فَبوُسْعي أَنْ أَكونَ كَما
تَرَكْتِني أَمس ، قُرْبَ الماء ، مُنْقَسِما
إلى سماءٍ وأَرْضٍ . آه . . . . أَينَ هُما؟

الجمعة : شتاءٌ آخر

إذا ذَهَبْتِ بَعيدًا ، عَلِّقي حُلمي
على الخِزانة ذكرى مِنْكِ ، أَو ذكرى
مِنِّي . سَيأتي شتاءٌ آخرُ ، وأَرى
حَمامَتَيْنِ على الكُرْسِيِّ ، ثُمَّ أرى
ماذا صَنَعْتُ بجَوْزِ الهند : من لُغَتي
سالَ الحليبُ على سُجَّادةٍ أُخرى

إذا ذهبْتِ ، خُذي فصل الشتاء ، إذًا!

[167]

Saturday: The Dove's Wedding

Listen to my body: Bees have their gods
Neighs have countless fiddles
I am the clouds. You are the earth, held against
a fence by the eternal wail of desire
Listen to my body: death has its fruits
and life has a life that renews itself only
from a body . . . that listens to a body

Sunday: The Melody of the *Nahawand*

He loves you. Come closer like a cloud . . . Come closer
to the stranger sobbing over me at the window:
I love her. Descend like a star . . . Descend
upon the traveler so that he'll stay on the road:
I love you. Spread out like darkness. Spread out
inside the lover's red rose and hesitate
like a tent. Hesitate, in the solitude of the king . . .

السبت : زواجُ الحمام

أُصْغي إلى جَسَدي : للنَحْلِ آلهَةٌ
وللصهيل رَبَاباتٌ بلا عَدَد
أنا السحابُ ، وأنت الأَرضُ ، يُسْنِدُها
على السيّاج أنينُ الرَغْبَة الأَبديّ
أُصْغي إلى جَسَدي : للموت فاكِهَةٌ
وللحياة حياةٌ لا تُجَدِّدُها
إلاّ على جَسَدٍ . . . يَصغي إلى جَسَد

الأحد : مَقامُ النِهَوَنْد

يُحبُّكِ ، اقْتَربي كالغَيْمَة . . . اقتربي
مِنَ الغريب على الشُّبّاك يجهشُ بي :
أُحبُّها . انْحَدِري كالنَّجمة . . . انْحَدِري
على المُسَافِر كي يبقى على سَفَرٍ :
أُحبُّكِ . انْتشري كالعَتْمَة . . . انتشري
في وردة العاشق الحمراء ، وارْتَبِكي
كالخيمَة ، ارتبكي ، في عُزْلَة المَلِك . . .

[169]

Monday: *Muwashah*

I pass by your name when I'm alone
like a Damascene passing through Andalusia

Here lemon lit up for you the salt of my blood
And here a wind fell from a mare

I pass by your name. No army nor country
encircles me. As if I were the last of the guards
or a poet strolling within his thoughts . . .

الإثنين : مُوَشَّح

أَمُرُّ باسْمك ، إذْ أَخلُو إلى نَفْسِي
كما يَمُرُّ دَمَشْقِيٌّ بأَندَلُسِ

هُنا أضاءَ لَكَ الليمونُ مِلْحَ دَمِي
وههُنا ، وَقَعَتْ ريحٌ عن الفَرَسِ

أَمُرُّ باسْمك ، لا جَيْشٌ يُحاصِرُني
ولا بلادٌ . كأَنِّي آخِرُ الحَرَسِ
أو شاعرٌ يَتَمَشَّى في هواجِسِه . . .

VI.

The Curtain Fell

أَغلقوا المَشهد . . .

Bertolt Brecht's Testimony
before a Military Court
(1967)

Your Honor!
I am not a soldier
So what do you want from me now?
I have nothing to do with the claims of the court
The past rushed to the past, quickly . . .
without heeding a word I said
The war withdrew to a café to rest . . .
Your pilots returned safe and sound
And the sky broke up in my language, Your
Honor – and this is my personal affair –
but your subjects are dragging my sky behind them . . . delighted
They peer over my heart, and throw banana peels
in the well. They rush by quickly
They say: Good evening. Sometimes
They come into my courtyard . . . at ease
They fall asleep on the cloud of my sleep . . . reassured
They use my own words
in my place
to address my window and the summer sweating the scent of jasmine
They repeat my own dream
in my place
and cry, with my eyes, psalms of longing

شهادةٌ من برتولت بريخت
أمام مَحكمة عسكريّة
(١٩٦٧)

سيِّدي القاضي!
أنا لَستُ بجنديٍّ ،
فماذا تَطلبونَ الآنَ منِّي؟
وأنا لا شأْنَ لي في ما تقولُ المحكمةْ ،
ذَهبَ الماضي إلى الماضي سريعًا . . .
دونَ أَن يسمعَ منِّي كَلمةْ .
مَضتِ الحربُ إلى المقهى لترتاحَ . . .
وطيّارُوكَ عادوا سالمينْ
والسماءُ انكسرتْ في لُغَتي ، يا سيِّدي
القاضي – وهذا شأْني الشخصيُّ –
لكنَّ رعاياكَ يجرُّونَ سمائي خلفهُمْ . . . مبتهجينْ
ويُطِلُّونَ على قلبي ، ويرمون قشورَ الموز
في البئرِ . ويمضونَ أمامي مُسرعينْ
ويقولونَ : مساءُ الخير ، أحيانًا ،
ويأتونَ إلى باحة بيتي . . . هادئينْ
وينامُونَ على غَيمة نَومي . . . آمنينْ
ويقولونَ كلامي نفسَهُ ،
بَدَلًا منِّي ،
لشُبَّاكي ، وللصَّيف الذي يَعْرَق عطرَ الياسمينْ
ويُعيدونَ منامي نفسَه ،
بَدَلًا منِّي ،
ويَبكون بعينيَّ مزاميرَ الحَنينْ

and sing, like I sang, to the olive and fig trees
to the part and the whole, in the buried meaning.
They live my life as they please
in my place
and walk carefully over my name . . .
And I, Your Honor, am here
in the hall of the past, a prisoner
The war is over. Your officers returned safe and sound
The vines spread in my language, Your
Honor – and this is my personal affair – when
the prison cell closes in on me, the earth stretches out to me
But your subjects sound out my words, angrily
They cry to Ahab and Jezebel: Stand up, inherit
the precious garden of Naboth!
They say: God is ours
and the land of God
is not for others!
What do you want, Your Honor,
from a passerby amidst passersby?
In a country where the executioner demands
that his victims praise his medals!
The time has come for me to scream
and to tear from my voice the mask of the word:
This is a prison cell, Your Honor, not a court
I am the witness and the judge. You are the defendant
Get out of your seat and go: You're free, you're free,
oh imprisoned judge

ويُغنُّونَ ، كما غنَّيْتُ للزَّيتون والتّين
وللجزئيِّ والكُلّيِّ في المَعنى الدَّفينْ .
ويَعيشون حياتي مثلما تعجبُهُمْ ،
بَدَلاً مِنّي ،
ويَمشون على اسمي حَذِرينْ . . .
وأنا ، يا سيِّدي القاضي هُنا
في قاعة الماضي ، سجينْ
مَضَت الحربُ . وضُبَّاطُك عادوا سالمينْ
والكرومُ انتشرتْ في لغَتي ، يا سيِّدي
القاضي – وهذا شأنيَ الشخصيُّ – إنْ
ضاقَتْ بيَ الزّنزانةُ امتدَّتْ بيَ الأرضُ ،
ولكنَّ رعاياك يجُسُّون كلامي غاضبينْ
ويَصيحُونَ بآخابَ وإيزابيلَ : قُوما ، وَرِثا
بستانَ نابوتَ الثَّمينْ!
ويقولون : لنا اللهُ
وأرضُ اللهِ
لا للآخرينْ!
ما الذي تطلبه ، يا سيِّدي القاضي ،
من العابر بين العابرين؟
في بلادٍ يَطْلُبُ الجلّادُ فيها
من ضحاياهُ مديحَ الأَوسمةْ!
آنَ لي أن أصرُخَ الآنَ
وأن أُسْقِطَ عن صوتي قناعَ الكلمةْ :
هذه زنزانةٌ ، يا سيِّدي ، لا مَحْكمةْ
وأنا الشّاهدُ والقاضي . وأنتَ الهيئةُ المُتَّهمةْ
فاتركِ المقعَدَ ، واذهب : أنتَ حُرٌّ أنتَ حُرّْ ،
أيُّها القاضي السجينْ

Your pilots returned safe and sound
The sky broke up in my first language –
and this is my personal affair – so that
our dead will return to us, safe and sound!

إنَّ طياريكَ عادوا سالمينْ
والسماءَ انكسرتْ في لُغَتي الأُولَى –
وهذا شأنِيَ الشخصيُّ – كَي يرجعَ
موتانا إلينا – سالمينْ!

A Non-Linguistic Dispute with Imru' al-Qays

The curtain fell
leaving a crack open for us to return to the others
incomplete. We climbed up onto the movie screen
smiling, as one must
in the movies. We improvised a few words, for us prepared
in advance, sorry for the martyrs'
last chance. Then we leaned down to submit
our names to those walking on either side. And we returned
to our tomorrow, incomplete . . .

The curtain fell
They were victorious
They crossed our entire yesterday
They forgave
the victim his sins when he apologized in advance
for whatever came to mind
They replaced time's bell
and were victorious

When they brought us to the penultimate act
we glanced back: smoke
towering over time, white over the gardens

خِلافٌ ، غيرُ لُغوِيّ ، مع امرئ القيس

أغلقوا المَشهَدَ
تاركِينَ لنا فُسحَةً للرّجوع إلى غَيرِنا
ناقِصِينَ . صَعِدْنا على شاشة السينما
باسِمِينَ ، كما يَنْبَغي أن نكونَ على
شاشة السّينما ، وارْتَجَلْنا كلامًا أعَدَّ
لنا سَلَفًا ، أَسفين على فُرْصَةِ
الشّهداء الأخيرة . ثمّ انْحَنَيْنا نُسَلِّمُ
أسماءَنا للمُشَاة على الجانبين . وعُدْنا
إلى غَدِنا ناقِصِينْ . . .

أغلقوا المَشهَدَ
انتصروا
عَبَرُوا أمسَنا كُلَّهُ ،
غَفَرُوا
للضحِيَّة أخطاءَها عندما اعتذَرَت
عَنْ كلام سيخطُرُ في بالها ،
غيَّروا جَرَسَ الوقتِ
وانتصروا . . .

عندما أوْصَلُونا إلى الفَصْل قبلَ الأَخير
التَفَتْنَا إلى الخلف : كانَ الدخانُ
يُطِلُّ مِنَ الوقتِ أبيضَ فوقَ الحدائق

behind us. Peacocks spread their fans
of colors across Caesar's edict to those who repent
over the worn-out vocabulary. The description of freedom
that didn't find its bread. A bread
without the salt of freedom. Or praise of doves
flying away from the market . . .
Caesar's edict was champagne for the smoke
that rose from time's balcony
white . . .

The curtain fell
They were victorious
They filmed what they wanted of our skies
one star . . . then another
They filmed what they wanted of our days
one cloud, then another
They replaced time's bell
and were victorious . . .

We saw ourselves playing in color on the reel
But we didn't find a star in the north or a tent
in the south. And we didn't recognize our own voice
That day our blood didn't speak into
the microphone. That day when we leaned against a language
that shredded its heart as it changed paths. No one

من بَعْدِنا . والطواويسُ تنشُرُ مروحةَ
اللَّون حول رسالة قَيْصَر للتائِينَ
عن المُفْرَدات التي اهتَرَأتْ . مثلاً :
وَصْفُ حُرِّيَة لم تجِدْ خُبْزَها . وَصْفُ
خُبْز بلا مِلْح حُرِّيَة . أو مَديحُ حمام
يطيرُ بعيدًا عَن الشَّوق . . .
كانت رسالةُ قَيْصَرَ شمبانيا للدخان
الذي يتصاعَدُ من شُرْفَة الوقت
أبيض . . .

أغلقوا المَشْهَدَ
انتصَروا
صَوَّروا ما يريدونَهُ من سماواتنا
نجمةً . . . نجمةً
صَوَّروا ما يريدونه من نهاراتنا
غيمةً غيمةً ،
غَيَّروا جَرَسَ الوقت
وانتصَروا . . .

إلتفتنا إلى دَوْرِنا في الشَّريط المُلوَّن ،
لكنَّنا لَم نَجِدْ نجمةً للشِّمال ولا خيمةً
للجنوب . ولم نَتَعَرَّفْ على صوتِنا أبَدًا .
لم يكُن دَمُنا يتكَلَّمُ في الميكروفونات في
ذلك اليوم ، يَوْمَ اتَّكَأْنا على لُغَةٍ

asked Imru' al-Qays: What have you done
to us, and to yourself? So go the way of
Caesar, behind the smoke that towers over
time, black. Go the way of
Caesar, alone, alone, alone
and leave us, here, your language!

بَعْثَرَتْ قلبها عندما غيَّرتْ دَرْبَها . لَم
يَقُلْ أَحدٌ لامرئ القيس : ماذا صنعتَ
بنا وبنفسكَ؟ فاذهبْ على درب
قَيْصَرَ ، خلف دُخان يُطلُّ منَ
الوقت أَسْوَدَ . واذْهَبْ على درب
قَيْصَرَ ، وَحْدَكَ ، وَحْدَكَ ، وَحْدَكَ
واتركْ لنا ، هُهُنا ، لُغَتَكْ!

Sequences for Another Time

A hasty day. I listen to the water
that the past takes away as it rushes by
Down below
I see myself split in two:
my name
and I . . .

I don't need anything to dream: a little bit
of sky for my visits is enough to see
time, light and familiar
around the doves' towers

A bit of the speech of God for the trees
is enough for me to build with words
a safe shelter
for the cranes that the hunter missed . . .

How my memory had to preserve
the names. How often I misspell
verbs. But this star is
my handiwork in marble . . .

مُتَتاليات لزمنٍ آخر

كانَ يومًا مُسْرِعًا . أنصتُّ للماء
الذي يأخُذُهُ الماضي ويمضي مُسْرِعًا ،
تَحْتَ ،
أَرَى نفسيَ تَنْشَقُّ إلى إثنينِ :
أنا ،
واسمي . . .

لكي أَحلُم لا يلزمُني شيءٌ : قليلٌ
من سماءٍ لزياراتي سيكفي لأَرَى
الوقتَ خفيفًا وأليفًا
حَوْلَ أبراجِ الحمامْ

وقليلٌ من كلامِ اللهِ للأَشجار
يكفيني لكي أَبنيَ بالألفاظِ
مأوى آمنًا
للكراكيِّ التي أخطأَها الصيّادُ . . .

كَمْ كانَ على ذاكرتي أَن تحفَظَ
الأَسماءَ . كَمْ أخطأتُ في تَهْجِيَةِ
الأَفعال . لكنْ هذه النجمةُ من
صُنْعِ يدي فوقَ الرَّخامْ . . .

A hasty day. No one apologized
to anyone. The clouds in the
tall trees didn't fall on the street
And blood didn't shine on the words

All is calm at the fork of the two rivers
From now on the days are without a history
There are neither living nor dead. There's no truce
Neither war waged against us, nor peace

My life is elsewhere. It's not important
to describe a café, or a conversation between two abandoned
windows. It's not important to describe an autumn chewing
gum in this crowd

. . . I don't need a spacious house to
dream. A little of the wolf's dozing
in the forest is enough to see, up high
a sky for my visits . . .

My life is elsewhere. It's not important
that the daughter of Genghis Khan, in her nightgown, see it
Or that a reader see it penetrate meaning
the way ink penetrates darkness

كانَ يومًا مُسْرِعًا . لم يَعْتَذِرْ
أَحَدٌ مِن أَحَدٍ فيه . ولم يسقُطْ
على الشَّارع غيمُ الشجر العالي
ولم يَلْمَعُ دَمٌ فوق الكلامْ

كلُ شيء هادِئٌ في مُلْتَقَى البَحْرَين
لا تاريخَ للأيّام مُنذ اليوم ،
لا موتى ولا أَحياءَ . لا هُدْنَةَ ،
لا حَرْبَ علينا أو سلامْ

وحياتي في مكان آخر . ليس مُهِمًّا
وَصْفُ مقهى وحوارٌ بين شُبَّاكَيْن
مَهْجُورَيْن . أو وَصْفٌ خريفٌ يَضَعُ
العِلْكَةَ في هذا الزحامْ

. . .ولكي أحلُمَ لا يلزَمُني بَيْتٌ
كبيرٌ . فقليلٌ من نُعاس الذئب
في الغابة يكفي لأَرى ، فوقَ ،
سماءً لزياراتي . . .

حياتي في مكان آخر . ليس مُهِمًّا
أن تراها بنتُ جنكيزخانَ في سروالِها
أو يراها قارِئٌ تدخُلُ في المعنَى
كما يدخُلُ حبرٌ في الظَّلامْ

A hasty day. The day after was a past
coming home from a tea party. The day after, we were!
The emperor was pleasant with us. We were
a day after . . . witnesses to the dedication of ruins . . .

All is calm. It's not important
to describe two blacksmiths who don't listen to
the tango. Or the dead sleeping, how
they sleep, without apologizing to their Highness, History . . .

I don't need a night like this to dream . . .
A little bit of sky for my visits is enough
to see time, light
and familiar,
and to sleep . . .

كان يومًا مُسرِعًا . والغَدُ ماضٍ
قادمٌ من حفلة الشّاي . غدًا كُنّا!
وكان الإمبراطورُ لطيفًا مَعنا . كُنّا
غدًا . . . نشهَدُ تدشينَ الرُّكامْ . . .

كُلُّ شيء هادئٌ . ليس مُهمًّا
وَصفُ حدّادينَ لم يُصغُوا إلى
التانْجُو ، ولا موتى ينامون ، كما
ناموا ولَم يَعْتَذِروا للسيّد التاريخ . . .

كي أَحلُم ، لا يلزمُني لَيْلٌ كهذا . . .
وقليلٌ من سماء لزياراتي ، سَيَكفي
لأَرى الوقتَ خفيفًا ،
وأَليفًا ،
وأَنام . . .

. . . As He Draws Away

The enemy who drinks tea in our shack has
a mare in smoke, a daughter with
thick eyebrows, brown eyes, long
hair like a night of songs over her shoulders. Her image
doesn't leave him when he comes over to ask for tea. But he
doesn't speak to us about her evening chores, or about
a mare abandoned by songs at the top of a hill . . . /

. . . In our shack the enemy takes a rest from his gun,
leaving it on my grandfather's chair. He eats our bread
like a guest, dozes on
the wicker chair, caresses our cat's
fur. He always says to us:
Don't blame the victim!
Who is the victim? We ask him.
He answers: Blood that the night will never dry . . . /

. . . The buttons on his uniform sparkle as he draws away.
Good evening to you! Say hello to our well
and to our fig trees. Tread gently on
our shadow in the barley fields. Say hello, higher up, to
our pines. Don't forget to lock the gate

للعدُوِّ الذي يشربُ الشَّايَ في كوخِنا
فَرَسٌ في الدخان . وبنتٌ لها
حاجبانِ كثيفانِ . عينانِ بُنِّيتانِ . وشَعْرٌ
طويلٌ كَلَيلِ الأغاني على الكَتِفَيْنِ . وصورتُها
لا تفارقُهُ كُلَّما جاءَنا يطلُبُ الشَّايَ . لكنَّهُ
لا يُحَدِّثُنا عن مشاغِلِها في المساء ، وعَنْ
فَرَسٍ تَرَكَتْهُ الأغاني على قِمَّةِ التَّلِ . . ./

. . . في كوخِنا يستريحُ العَدُوُّ من البُندقيَّةِ ،
يتُرُكُها فوقَ كُرسيِّ جَدِّي . ويأكُلُ من خُبزِنا
مثلما يفعَلُ الضيفُ . يَغفو قليلاً على
مقعدِ الخَيْزُرانِ . ويَحنُو على فَرْوِ
قِطَّتِنا . ويقولُ لنا دائمًا :
لا تلوموا الضحيَّةَ!
نسألُهُ : مَنْ هيَ؟
فيقولُ : دَمٌ لا يُجَفِّفُهُ اللّيلُ . . ./

. . . تلمعُ أزرارُ سُتْرتِه عندما يبتعدْ
عِمْ مساءً! وسَلِّمْ على بئرِنا
وعلى جِهَةِ التِّينِ . وامشِ الهُوَيْنى على
ظِلِّنا في حقولِ الشَّعيرِ . وسَلِّمْ على سَرْوِنا
في الأعالي . ولا تَنْسَ بوّابةَ البيتِ مفتوحةً

[193]

at night. Don't forget the horse's
fear of airplanes
And greet us, there, if time allows . . . /

These words that we'd wished
to say at the door . . . he hears them,
hears them well, but hides them in a quick cough
and tosses them aside
So why does he visit the victim every evening?
And memorize our proverbs, like us?
And repeat our songs of
our own appointments in the holy place?
Were it not for the gun
the flute would pass into the flute . . . /

. . . The war will last as long as the earth
in us revolves around itself!
Let's be good then. He used to ask us
to be good. He'd read the verses
of Yeats' Airman: Those that I fight
I do not hate, those that I guard
I do not love . . .
Then he'd leave our wooden shack
and walk eighty meters to
our stone house, there, at the edge of the plain . . . /

في اللّيالي . ولا تَنْسَ خَوْفَ
الحِصان من الطائرات ،
وسَلِّمْ عَلينا ، هُناك ، إذا اتَّسَعَ الوَقتُ . . ./

هذا الكلامُ الذي كان في وُدِّنا
أن نقولَ على الباب . . . يَسْمَعُهُ جيّدًا
جيّدًا ، ويُخَبِّئُهُ في السُّعال السَّريع
ويُلْقي به جانبًا .
فلماذا يزورُ الضحيّةَ كُلَّ مساء؟
ويحفظُ أمثالَنا مثْلَنا ،
ويُعيدُ أناشيدَنا ذاتَها ،
عن مواعيدنا ذاتها في المكان المُقدَّس؟
لولا المسدسُ
لاختلطَ النّايُ في النّاي . . ./

. . . لنْ تنتهي الحربُ ما دامتِ الأَرضُ
فينا تدورُ على نفسها!
فلنَكُنْ طيّبين إذًا . كان يسألُنا
أن نكونَ هُنا طيّبين . ويقرأُ شعرًا
لطيّار «ييتْس» : أنا لا أُحبُّ الذينَ
أُدافعُ عنهُمْ ، كما أنني لا أُعادي
الذينَ أُحاربُهُمْ . . .
ثمّ يخرجُ من كوخنا الخشبيِّ ،
ويمشي ثمانينَ مترًا إلى
بيتنا الحجريِّ هُناك على طَرَف السَّهْلِ . . ./

Say hello to our house, stranger
Our coffee cups
are still as they were. Can you smell
our fingers on them? Will you tell your daughter with
her long braid and two thick eyebrows that she has
an absent friend
who would like to visit her? For nothing . . .
but to enter her mirror and see his secret:
How she follows, after him, the course of his life
in his place? Say hello to her
if time allows . . . /

These words that we'd wished
to say, he hears them,
hears them well
but hides them in a quick cough
and tosses them aside. The buttons
of his uniform sparkle as he draws away . . .

سَلِّمْ على بيتنا يا غريبُ .

فناجينُ

قهوتنا لا تزالُ على حالها . هل تَشُمُّ

أصابعَنَا فوقها؟ هل تقولُ لبنتك ذات

الجديلة والحاجبين الكثيفين إنَّ لها

صاحبًا غائبًا ،

يتمنَّى زيارَتَها ، لا لِشيْءٍ . . .

ولكنْ ليدخل مرآتَها ويرى سِرَّهُ :

كيفَ كانتْ تُتابعُ من بعده عُمْرَهُ

بدلاً منه؟ سَلِّمْ عليها

إذا اتَّسَع الوَقتْ . . . /.

هذا الكلامُ الذي كان في وُدِّنا

أَن نقولَ له ، كان يسمعُهُ جيِّدًا

جيِّدًا ،

ويُحبُّهُ في سُعَالٍ سريعٍ ،

ويُلْقَى به جانبًا ، ثمّ تلْمَعُ

أزرارُ سُتْرَتِه عندما يَبْتَعِدْ . . .

I write to defy oblivion.

—Mahmoud Darwish

This printing of *Why Did You Leave the Horse Alone?* was generously supported by an anonymous donor and by United Palestinian Appeal, Inc.

Established in 1978 as a not-for-profit, UPA empowers Palestinians to improve their lives and communities through socially responsible and sustainable programs in health, education, and community and economic development. UPA is a non-political and non-sectarian organization that operates from its headquarters in Washington, DC and its field offices in the West Bank, Gaza and the refugee camps in Jordan and Lebanon.